interpreting the
WILL OF GOD
principles for unlocking the mystery

D1607665

mack king carter

edited by jean alicia elster

Judson Press
Valley Forge

Interpreting the Will of God:
Principles for Unlocking the Mystery

Library of Congress Cataloging-in-Publication Data

Carter, Mack King.
      Interpreting the will of God : principles for unlocking the mystery / Mack King Carter.
            p.   cm.
      ISBN 0-8170-1424-1 (pbk. : alk. paper)
      1. Christian life 2. God—Will. I. Title.
BV4509.5 .C38   2002
248.4—dc21   2001050409

Printed in Canada.

08 07 06 05 04 03 02

10 9 8 7 6 5 4 3 2 1

CONTENTS

FOREWORD

ONE OF THE MOST CRUCIAL AND BEWILDERING DIMENSIONS OF the Christian faith is the notion that believers can know the will of God. Such a belief is crucial because if one can discern God's will, one is strengthened to act in harmony with the Creator of the universe. Then too, if we embody God's will, our lives can help address human suffering and enhance our pledge to be emissaries of divine order. But the will of God is surely one of the most confusing elements of Christian faith. After all, how can one be certain that one is doing God's will? How do we distinguish our own wish fulfillments and the projections of our human desire from God's will? And how do we avoid the pitfall of believing that we have unlimited and infallible access to God's will? What is the role of faith in the process of discovering God's will, and how reliable are Scripture and tradition in helping us to clarify God's intentions for us?

Thankfully, Dr. Mack King Carter helps to address these and other pressing questions that arise as we seek to understand God's will. Carter's book is all the more compelling because of his rigorous engagement with the theological sources of Christian belief. Too often, parish ministers are caught in the grind of crucial "housekeeping" chores—marriages, funerals, administrative tasks, prayer meetings, and church business—and find, or take, little time to study the faith. While we love God with our hearts and souls, we often forget to love God with our minds. Carter is exemplary in his devout attention to critical inquiry. His sermons are models of theological *gravitas*. His sacred rhetoric fairly teems with a profound wrestling with the weighty, and contradictory, matters of faith and reason. Carter has never been afraid to stretch his congregation's spiritual imagination and to lift its theological I.Q. through demanding preaching and teaching.

That trait stands out in his scholarly work as well, as evident in the structure of this book. Carter begins by meditating on the nature of God, tackling the huge question of divine identity before he leads us to systematically reflect on the various modes through which the will of God is revealed. Carter manages to embrace a Christ-centered vision of divine revelation while paying attention to supplementary elements of belief—with suffering, active patience, faith, fellowship, counsel, and common sense primary among them—that support our knowledge of what God intends. This critical textual and theological strategy prevents Carter from taking the easy way out of the sharp dilemmas posed by the attempt to discern God's will; in other words, by not simply saying, as the saw goes, that "God said it, I believe it, and that settles it." Carter's keen sensitivity to conflict, contradiction, even paradox in the Christian worldview allows him to balance biblical and cultural forces in detailing the route to understanding God's intentions for human beings.

An especially noteworthy feature of Carter's theological arsenal is what may be termed his structural sympathy for the victim of oppressive forces. His sympathy is structural because it is the basis of his philosophy of interpreting the Bible: we must link the landscape of sacred literature to the lives we live in the here and now. Unless God is able to meet the challenges of our existence—and unless the Bible can adequately address the hurt and terror of our frail humanity—then our beliefs are of little use. Carter's insistence that suffering is a key ingredient in the will of God is, in this light, even more important to his theological outlook. Carter intends no endorsement of sadistic beliefs in needless pain as the ground of our encounter with God. Instead, Carter aims to show that the unavoidable suffering we endure as human pilgrims can nonetheless illuminate, perhaps radiate, the will of God. This is not to valorize suffering. It is, instead, to transform it, as the best theological minds have done. The beauty of Carter's theology is that suffering—whether racial oppression or economic inequality—must be resisted even as its capacity to harm is challenged in the crucible of intelligent love.

We must not gloss over Carter's bold reckoning with what is known in formal theological terms as "theodicy," or the question of suffering and evil. As Rabbi Harold Kushner memorably phrased it, theodicy asks why "bad things happen to good people." While such ruminations have for centuries formed a category of theological reflection, it is particularly unpopular to raise such questions in too many contemporary pulpits. The gospel of wealth has gutted our theological courage and left a shell of spiritual enthusiasms that ultimately lack the power to revive us or to heal our deepest wounds. The sanctification of materialism as the breath of God has left a foul homiletical stench in pulpits across the nation. The parishioners of such congregations are spoon-fed a diet of biblical justifications for acquiring the trinkets of capitalism that leave them famished for more substantive moral fare. Carter's dive into the heart of these matters is not simply refreshing, but vitally necessary if we are to resist seeing consumer goods and creature comforts as the exclusive sign of God's blessing—and hence, of God's will for our lives. By insisting on a vigorous confrontation with suffering, Carter offers a mature theology that addresses the most acute challenges to Christian belief.

Interpreting the Will of God is particularly important as our nation grapples with the direction it should take in light of the tragedy of September 11, 2001. More than ever, we must seek to know what God intends for us as we grapple with the terror visited on us from outside our nation, and the terror we have poured on the heads of innocent folk both near and far. Mack King Carter's insightful treatise offers a helpful guide to seeking God's will and living our lives in the light of such knowledge. In this era of enormous spiritual and social crisis, nothing could be more valuable.

—Michael Eric Dyson, Ph.D.
The Avalon Foundation Professor of Humanities
Professor of Religious Studies
and Afro-American Studies
University of Pennsylvania
Philadelphia, Pennsylvania

ACKNOWLEDGMENTS

THIS BOOK IS DEDICATED TO THE MINISTERIAL INFLUENCES IN my life.

The Reverend Charles Henry Rhodes, 1867–1969, the pastor of the Calvary Baptist Church of Ocala, Florida, was my first influence. He was a man of great charisma and moral character. He was that bridge between the post-slavery preacher and the social revolution of the 1960s. He was the first preacher that I ever saw and heard.

The Reverend Alfred Deter Lonon, 1907–1978, the pastor of New Bethel Baptist Church of Ocala, Florida, was my pastor. He baptized me, licensed me, and ordained me to be a pastor-teacher. This charismatic man had a great insight into the psyche of oppressed people. As a preacher he was a powerful evangelist who was gifted with a great imagination. When I was just ten years old, he ordained me as a deacon and gave me great encouragement until his homecoming.

The Reverend Charles Pinkney "Pink" Brown, 1889–1971, pastor of the Mount Moriah Baptist Church of Ocala, Florida, without equivocation was one of the greatest preachers ever. Here was a man of Churchillian felicity in speech and a man of great homiletical and exegetical gifts. His intellectual power, as well as his ability to deliver the Word, gave awesome testimony to how great God is. He encouraged me to maximize my own gifts.

Doctor George Arthur Buttrick, 1892–1980, pastor of Madison Avenue Presbyterian Church of New York City, was one of Christendom's greatest pulpiteers. Any book on preaching must consider his contribution or we must declare the publication irrelevant. He was my professor of homiletics at Southern Baptist Theological Seminary in Louisville, Kentucky. I was his student assistant and was privileged to be one of the eulogizers at his memorial service in January 1980. My mind was stretched because of his high standards for the ministry of proclamation.

Doctor George Edward Weaver, 1921–, pastor emeritus of the New Mount Olive Baptist Church of Fort Lauderdale, Florida, was my predecessor at this great preaching station. Dr. Weaver, whom I affectionately call "Daddy," is a man of great vision, pulpit power, and character. It was my privilege to serve with him as copastor of the New Mount Olive Baptist Church from 1981 to 1982. Upon his retirement, I was called to be his successor. The beautiful relationship that we have, characterized by great love and sincere civility for each other, continues to be a model for the nation.

The Reverend Lewis Napoleon Anderson, 1880–1974, was the pastor of the Mount Moriah Baptist Church of Ocala, Florida. Rev. Anderson was a gifted teacher of the gospel. His emphasis upon the task of the pastor-teacher continues to inspire and challenge me even today.

The Reverend Oliver Van Pinkston, 1905–, is the pastor emeritus of the Covenant Misionary Baptist Church of Ocala, Florida. He has played an integral part in my life and in the life of my family. He is known as a Baptist statesman and a gifted Bible expositor. Beyond this, he served on my ordination council, preached the ordination sermon, performed our wedding in 1973, and presided at our twenty-fifth anniversary in 1998. For him we say "to God be the glory."

Doctor Martin Luther King Sr., 1899–1984, or "Daddy King" as he was known across the world, was the father of Dr. Martin Luther King Jr. The fire that burned in the heart of his son first burned within him. Like his son, he was also a kamikaze for justice. His life was a blessing to me, from a distance and close up. He never failed to encourage me to continue to blow the prophetic trumpet. In February 1983 he preached my installation sermon at New Mount Olive. For all that he gave to the world, and to me, we give thanks.

The Reverend Jesse Ernest McCrary, 1913–1982, was the pastor of the Hopewell Baptist Church of Ocala, Florida, and later served as the pastor of Truevine Baptist Church of Sarasota, Florida. Although I was never a member of his congregation, his gift as a pastoral-evangelist greatly influenced my life. His pulpit power was greatly heralded. He was one of the South's greatest revivalists.

INTRODUCTION

ONE OF THE GREATEST CHALLENGES FACING CHRISTIANS TODAY is determining the will of God in their lives. Because we live in a world in which advertisements, television, radio talk shows, videos, song lyrics, and countless other influences seek to control the decisions we make, it has become more difficult than ever before to know God's plan for us.

Interpreting the Will of God gives readers the tools necessary to look beyond the influences that compete for their attention and to focus on the Lord's plan for them. Each chapter offers a key that allows believers and seekers alike to effectively interpret God's will for their lives.

Chapter 1 establishes the foundation of this book by exploring the nature and characteristics of God. Only by understanding these holy attributes can we begin to see the divine will at work in our lives. Chapter 2 surveys the three basic types of God's will: *intentional, circumstantial, and ultimate.* These three categories are used throughout the remaining chapters to describe God's will.

In chapter 3 we examine Jesus of Nazareth. Since he is the embodiment and the face of God, we must examine his life and teachings in order to know what God would have us do in our own lives. Chapter 4 looks at suffering as it relates to interpreting the will of God. While acknowledging that suffering can be a tremendous impediment to a clear understanding of God's will, this chapter lays claim to, and then proves, that God's will can indeed be made known through suffering.

Failure and rejection become life-affirming attributes when we are considering the will of God in our lives. Chapter 5 shows how failure and rejection are preludes to a deeper relationship with God, spiritual victory, and other tremendous windows of opportunity as we seek to know God's will. Chapter 6 considers patience and the profound benefits we receive when we wait to know the will of God. Patience, rather than being passive and inactive, is shown to be a vibrant, dynamic opportunity for growth in our spiritual lives.

Chapter 7 examines faith as a means of surrendering to God's will. It looks, from a fresh viewpoint, at several Old and New Testament examples of faith. In addition, this chapter considers how to increase our faith as we seek to discern God's will.

Fellowship with God is the focus of chapter 8. Starting with the basic premise that we are better able to know God's will through increased fellowship with the Almighty, this chapter explores powerful ways in which we can experience this fellowship. Then, chapter 9 exhorts us to know God's will by considering the input of others through discussion. It provides a consideration of various situations in which discussion and outside input are essential to learning the will of God.

Finally, in chapter 10 the connection between common sense and understanding God's will is explored through a refreshing question-and-answer format. The answers to these thought-provoking questions solidify the base of knowledge presented in the entire book.

Through the information and the spiritual insights contained within these ten chapters, it is my hope that *Interpreting the Will of God* will provide readers with keys for knowing God's plan for their lives and having the confidence to accept the divine will.

CHAPTER 1

Understanding the Nature of God

ANY GUIDELINES FOR INTERPRETING THE WILL OF GOD MUST begin with a proper understanding of the nature of God. For when we know the nature, or characteristics, of God, we know who God is. And knowing this is one of the keys to unlocking the mystery of the divine will.

Who God Is

First and foremost, we know that God is the supreme creator, sustainer, and ruler of the universe. From the very first verse of the Bible, Genesis 1:1, we know that God is not just God of this earth, but of all the heavens. In fact, "the highest heavens belong to the LORD" (Psalm 115:16). In other words, God's reach extends not just to those heavenly bodies that can be seen with the most powerful telescopes that have been sent spiraling through the heavens, but also to the undiscovered, unseen places of the universe. This is a God who knows no boundaries, who cannot be contained.

Then we know that there are attributes, or qualities, that belong only to God.

God is the Eternal Spirit. Having no tangible body, God cannot be confined by time and space.

God is love. It is an incontestable biblical truth that the Judeo-Christian God is love (1 John 4:8). Yet, this love is not a doting sentimentality. As described in Hebrews 12:6-8, it includes discipline, chastisement, correction, and hardship. In today's vernacular, we would call it "tough love." In the short run it may hurt us, but in the long run it will help us. We might compare this love to childhood immunization shots, which are painful but prevent the occurrence of debilitating and even deadly diseases.

God is omnipotent. God is the Almighty (Revelation 1:8). In the Old Testament, a common name of God is El Shaddai, or God Almighty. Here, God is revealed as being the one with the power to accomplish all that he promises to do. In the New Testament, this power manifests itself through Jesus' resurrection and victory over death.

God is omnipresent. God cannot be restricted by human boundaries such as nationality, gender, and race. God is above us and yet with us, inhabiting all situations and circumstances. Unlike the "local" deities of the ancient Israelites' neighbors, God is present with and without the creation, from now and throughout eternity (Matthew 28:20b).

God is omniscient. God knows all things. This is in contrast to human knowledge, which is fragmented. We learn new things and forget others. We know some things well but nothing completely. God's knowledge is complete: "He knows everything" (1 John 3:20b).

God is faithful. God will not forsake us. We can trust God, for "he who promised is faithful" (Hebrews 10:23).

God is holy. Holiness describes the nature of God in relation to humanity. God alone is worthy to be worshiped and praised, for he represents all that is sacred. Because of sin, human character is flawed. We can never equal the stature of God. Scripture makes this point clear. When God speaks to Moses, Moses hides his face because he is afraid to look at

God (Exodus 3:6). The prophet Isaiah cries, "Woe is me. . . . I am a man of unclean lips," when he comes face to face with God (Isaiah 6:5).

God is righteous. God is just and fair. Psalm 11:7 says, "For the LORD is righteous, he loves justice." Therefore, God does not leave Isaiah in his misery. God takes away Isaiah's sin and calls him as prophet. In the same way, God the Father, in his righteousness, sent his Son to die for the sins of all humanity. God thereby makes it possible for us to hear and to act upon the divine call on our lives.

God is merciful. Sin causes God to frown, but merciful encounters cause a smile to light up God's face. "The LORD was grieved that he had made man on the earth, and his heart was filled with pain. So the LORD said, 'I will wipe mankind, whom I have created, from the face of the earth . . . for I am grieved that I have made them.' But Noah found favor in the eyes of the LORD" (Genesis 6:6-8). In spite of God's grief over humankind's depravity, Noah gave God a reason to smile again. Then, after the disaster of the deluge in Genesis 7–8, God moved in compassion and mercy to help Noah and his family rebuild. The same is true when we accept God's offer of mercy. God is more than elated, and God is there to direct and sustain us as we rebuild our lives.

God is truth. People may try to tell the truth, but God is truth (1 John 5:6; cf. John 17:17). Truth is at the core of the divine nature. God cannot lie. Even when we misrepresent God, he remains true.

God is sovereign. This sovereignty means that God is in control of both order and chaos (Psalm 103:19). No principalities, powers, or persons will ever defeat God, who not only is in control, but is actively directing all things toward their appointed goal.

God is immutable. God never moves in contradiction to the nature of the divine will. All that God was, he still is; all that God is, he will be (Exodus 3:14; Malachi 3:6; cf. Hebrews 13:8). Therefore, there is constancy in life and in the universe.

God is great. Even though humankind lives in the realm of deceit and violence, God operates at a higher level. God's greatness leaps far beyond the bounds of human expression, and it means that he alone is worthy to be praised. No human being is to be worshiped. "Great is the LORD, and most worthy of praise. . . . For this God is our God for ever and ever; he will be our guide even to the end" (Psalm 48:1,14).

In understanding God's will, it is important that we take into consideration that God is above every other so-called god. God is great in that the public manifestation of morality is in line with the divine nature. God cannot be restricted in his love for the entire world. God's name is to be exalted and proclaimed among all peoples. "My name will be great among the nations, from the rising to the setting of the sun" (Malachi 1:11).

God is eternal. This eternity means that God is both the beginning and the end (Revelation 1:8). The essence of God's being is self-contained. Nothing outside of God can cause divine being or nonbeing. Like a circle, God has no point of origin. God is, and always will be.

What God Does

Along with understanding that God's nature provides an important basis for knowing God and for interpreting the divine will, it is equally as important to examine the *works* of God: those things that God does and that occur because of who God is. These, like all descriptions of God, are windows that shed light upon and help us interpret the divine will. Just as we began our examination of the nature of God with the characteristic of creator of the universe, so too must we acknowledge that of all the works of God, the first and foremost is the work of God as creator.

God creates. "In the beginning" of Genesis 1:1 is the foundation of the Judeo-Christian faith. This passage teaches us that God took the initiative in the drama of creation. Once the basis of this creative work was completed, God commanded humankind to live at an exalted level above the creation but subordinate to God (Genesis 1:26-30). This is significant and essential to any understanding of the will of God. We are to live out our lives with a responsibility to all of creation. The fact that God created humankind with this kind of dominion speaks to the importance of our role in the maintenance of creation. It also suggests that if we can have this sort of relationship with the rest of creation, then it is imperative that we maintain relationships with each other. To do any less is contrary to God's will.

God speaks. While none of us can ever hope to obtain a perfect understanding of God's will, we cannot know anything about it until God speaks. In Genesis 1:3, God begins to speak. And, since creation came about as a result of this speaking, we see clearly that there is power in the divine Word.

Yet, while God can talk to the creation without frustration, the ultimate conversation is God's dialogue with humankind. "In the past God spoke to our forefathers through the prophets at many times and in various ways, but in these last days he has spoken to us by his Son" (Hebrews 1:1-2). Just think of it: God communicates with us! Our God is not like the idols seen in the Old Testament, made of "wood and stone, of silver and gold" (Deuteronomy 29:17), which could not speak. The Bible states unequivocally that our God not only speaks but also can be spoken to. "The righteous cry out, and the LORD hears them" (Psalm 34:17). God's words become light and life for us. To hear and to know God's Word is to be in line with the divine will.

God brings life. Once again, the verses of Genesis 1 describe God in the creating of all living things. After creating plants and trees, God brings forth birds and sea creatures, and then all of the animals of the earth. Life exists abundantly in the air and water and upon the land. God's greatest commitment to life, however, is demonstrated in this text:

> Then God said, "Let us make man in our image, in our likeness, and let them rule over the fish of the sea and the birds of the air, over the livestock, over all the earth, and over all the creatures that

move along the ground." So God created man in his own image, in the image of God he created him; male and female he created them. God blessed them and said to them, "Be fruitful and increase in number; fill the earth and subdue it." (Genesis 1:26-28)

These Scripture verses point out the fact that from the beginning, God's view of life is deep and expansive. The "life challenges" of the twenty-first century such as abortion, capital punishment, and the protection of plants and animals within their environments have become trivialized as political issues. But, simply put in Scripture, God's will is for all life forms to exist. God is on the side of life.

God blesses. God's will is for people to be blessed. The blessings of God are a reward for those who live in the divine will (Matthew 5:3-12). These blessings flow from creation, through the incarnate Christ, and into the covenant community. However, God does not want us simply to collect blessings and hoard them for ourselves. God blesses us in order that we might be a blessing to others. In Genesis 12:2-3, the LORD says to Abraham, "I will make you into a great nation and I will bless you; I will make your name great, and you will be a blessing. I will bless those who bless you, and whoever curses you I will curse; and all peoples on earth *will be blessed through you"* (emphasis added).

We see clearly from this passage that it is the will of God for us to be conduits of divine blessings. It is never God's intention that we keep the blessings for ourselves. God's plan is a world-encompassing vision. We are here to be blessed and, in turn, to be a blessing to others.

God sanctifies. We have already noted that God is holy; God also can sanctify people and situations and thereby make them holy (Hebrews 2:11). What God touches is set apart, or sanctified, for God's use and glory. By such sanctification, the Lord set apart the prophet Jeremiah before he was even born (Jeremiah 1:4-5). After the work of creation was completed, God blessed the seventh day, making it holy. Therefore, it is God's will that we, and the situations in our lives, be exclusively surrendered to the divine purpose for our lives. God's will is that we, as the people of God, live lives of total surrender.

God sees. While God's omniscience refers to knowing all things, the fact that God "sees" refers to a specific focus on the human situation. In Genesis 16:13, our African sister Hagar, after being kicked out of the household of Abraham at the instigation of Sarah, speaks rather forthrightly in declaring that in spite of her situation, she is still under the surveillance of God. "She gave this name to the LORD who spoke to her: 'You are the God who sees me,' for she said, 'I have now seen the One who sees me.'"

In other words, our particular dilemmas cannot block God's vision. God sees us. This is further declared in the New Testament. God's seeing us is not a cold and callous look, but a look of love.

> Are not two sparrows sold for a penny? Yet not one of them will fall to the ground apart from the will of your Father. And even the very hairs on your head are all numbered. So, don't be afraid; you are worth more than many sparrows. (Matthew 10:29-31)

What an insight into understanding the will of God! These passages declare that in the entire universe, we are at the top of God's agenda. God sees all and is prepared to act on our behalf.

God rests.

> By the seventh day God had finished the work he had been doing; so on the seventh day he rested from all his work. And God blessed the seventh day and made it holy, because on it he rested from all the work of creating that he had done. (Genesis 2:2-3)

It is a great inspiration to believers everywhere when we discover that God rested only after perfectly completing the work of creation. After order and purpose had been established, and after humankind had been given the task of being God's manager of creation, then God rested. We must learn at the human level that what is done is done. We are not God, but there is a message for us as we live our lives believing that what God wills for our lives is good. After doing our best, we must rest in knowing that what could be done has been done; therefore, we move on. We must always keep a balance between working and resting. Those who work but do not rest will live lives of great frustration; those who rest but never work are already defeated.

God permits evil to exist. In Genesis 3:1-7, the serpent assails Eve and Adam in the garden of Eden.

> Now the serpent was more crafty than any of the wild animals the LORD God had made. He said to the woman, "Did God really say, 'You must not eat from any tree in the garden'?" The woman said to the serpent, "We may eat fruit from the trees in the garden, but God did say, 'You must not eat fruit from the tree that is in the middle of the garden, and you must not touch it, or you will die.'" "You will not surely die," the serpent said to the woman. "For God knows that when you eat of it your eyes will be opened, and you will be like God, knowing good and evil." When the woman saw that the fruit of the tree was good for food and pleasing to the eye, and also desirable for gaining wisdom, she took some and ate it. She also gave some to her husband, who was with her, and he ate it. Then the eyes of both of them were opened.

This is one of the most difficult and perplexing texts in the Bible because it seems to impale God on the horns of a dilemma. Did God, who is good, create evil? If not, where did evil come from? It is amazing that the Bible never seeks to extricate God either from absurdity or from apparent contradictions. However, human freedom, or free will, is the classic Christian response to this incident in the garden because the serpent had no power over the first couple. They chose to do what they did. At any time, they could have rejected the serpent's overtures. But their failure to do so opened up a floodgate of evil and rebellion against God, humanity, and the environment.

We believe that God is not the cause of evil. Yet we declare that God is responsible for evil, not because the serpent was created to sin but was created with the potential for evil and good. All conscious creation is given the same freedom to choose. Therefore, the dilemma remains, but God is great both in spite of it and because of it.

God judges sin. It is undeniable that there is a penalty to be paid for rebelling against God. When humankind succumbed to the seductive wiles of the serpent, God, as Genesis 3:14-19 shows, was prepared to render judgment. This judgment in Genesis 3:14-19 is fourfold, none of which was intended by God in creation (see Genesis 1–2).

First, God curses the serpent to perpetual warfare with humanity. Then God says to the woman, "I will greatly increase your pains in childbearing; with pain you will give birth to children. Your desire will be for your husband, and he will rule over you." In this judgment, the woman is not only assured of pain in the delivery of offspring but also is now subordinated in her relationship with her husband.

Third, God says to the man,

Because you listened to your wife and ate from the tree . . . , Cursed is the ground because of you; through painful toil you will eat of it all the days of your life. It will produce thorns and thistles for you. . . . By the sweat of your brow you will eat your food until you return to the ground, since from it you were taken; for dust you are and to dust you will return.

In the judgment against the man, God does not curse him with work, because having dominion already encompasses tremendous amounts of work. The judgment is that the man must do work that is painful and unenjoyable. To be involved in any vocation that does not bring fulfillment is to revisit the curse of Adam. The tedium of work is the curse. Therefore, it is God's will that we be involved in vocations that will bless us, and others, to God's glory. The second aspect of this curse is that the man (both as an individual and as a representative of all humanity) will experience physical death. This is not to say that if humankind had not sinned we would have lived forever in our current physical state. Rather, it is reasonable to believe that we would have been transformed into a higher dimension of life, as was the case with Enoch (Genesis 5:24) and with Elijah (2 Kings 2:11). The curse is not so much in leaving this life as having to deal with the anticipation, anxiety, and finality of death.

Fourth, the environment, or the natural order, becomes hostile to the interests of humanity. Nature both blesses and curses. "Cursed is the ground because of you; through painful toil you will eat of it all the days of your life. It will produce thorns and thistles for you."

These verdicts upon humanity clearly establish God as judge. However, the judgment of God is neither malicious nor vindictive. God is righteous (Psalm 50:6). It is not God's will that we live lives of moral rebellion, but when we do rebel, divine judgment will prevail.

God grieves and feels anger. "The LORD was grieved that he had made man on the earth, and his heart was filled with pain. So the LORD said, 'I will wipe mankind, whom I have created, from the face of the earth—men and animals, and creatures that move along the ground, and birds of the air—for I am grieved that I have made them'" (Genesis 6:6-7).

The Judeo-Christian God is not like the gods of Greek and Roman mythology. As the Creator and the One in whose image we are made, our God feels the pain and anger of grief. This Scripture in no way serves as a confession that God made a mistake in creating humankind. God does not regret the decision of creation but rather grieves the way in which humanity has perverted the creation.

Another expression of God's anger is expressed in dismay with the Hebrews in the wilderness. Here again, God responds to the attitude of the transgressor.

> Do not harden your hearts as you did in the rebellion during the time of testing in the desert, where your fathers tested and tried me and for forty years saw what I did. That is why I was angry with that generation, and I said, "Their hearts are always going astray, and they have not known my ways." So I declared on oath in my anger, "They shall never enter my rest." (Hebrews 3:8-11)

It is key to interpreting the will of God that we understand divine anger and grief not as God's state of mind but rather as God's response to humanity's attitude toward the moral bounds that he has set.

God welcomes discovery. It is not irreverent to say, "God has a lot of kid in him." The possibility and propensity for humankind to "discover" what God has already created amuses God to no end.

> The LORD had said to Abram, "Leave your country, your people and your father's household and go to the land I will show you. I will make you into a great nation and I will bless you; I will make your name great, and you will be a blessing. I will bless those who bless you, and whoever curses you I will curse; and all peoples on earth will be blessed through you." So Abram left, as the Lord had told him. (Genesis 12:1-4)

We can hear and feel the excitement in God's voice in challenging Abraham to discover a new land. Whenever we seek to be all that we can be intellectually, spiritually, morally, and socially, God is thrilled. However, our progress must be God-centered and human-related. We must view it as a blessing as God directs and develops the divine vision and will for our lives.

It is God's will that we make new discoveries without destroying human personality. One of the great fears of the twenty-first century is the deification of scientific discoveries. Whenever we deify the created rather than revere the deity of the Creator, we commit idolatry. It is not God's will for us to resort to such extremes. If science worships God and honors people through its discoveries, then that is a tremendous gift. If, however, it places human-directed scientific discovery above God-directed discovery, then we are faced with the unimaginable outcomes of procedures such as human cloning.

God protects us. God's protection is enabling (Deuteronomy 32:10-11). God protects us in order to make us sufficient enough to care for ourselves. It is not the divine will for

God to do for us what we have been enabled to do for ourselves. God's protection is not about a life of fantasy where we never encounter difficulties.

The story of the three Hebrew youths—Shadrach, Meshach, and Abednego—in Daniel 3 is instructive on this point. These three young men refused to bow down and worship the golden statue set up by King Nebuchadnezzar, even though they knew they would be thrown into a fiery furnace as punishment. Their reply to the king's personal command to worship the golden image provides a realistic and spiritually mature understanding of the nature of God's protection.

> "O Nebuchadnezzar," they replied, "we do not need to defend ourselves before you in this matter. If we are thrown into the blazing furnace, the God we serve is able to save us from it, and he will rescue us from your hand, O king. *But even if he does not, . . .* we will not serve your gods or worship the image of gold you have set up." (Daniel 3:16-18 [emphasis added])

As this episode illustrates, God's will does not mean protection from all of the challenges of life. God's protection is about sharing the divine victory while being firmly grounded in earthly realities.

God hears us. Biblically speaking, this is not about passive listening. It is about God answering prayer. The Judeo-Christian God is unlike any other god. This is the God who enters into dialogue with people and answers their petitions. Unlike the Phoenician god Baal, our God is able to hear or see. The God who hears and answers prayer is at the heart of biblical theology (Psalm 4:1; Zechariah 10:6). It is God's will to hear and answer our prayers.

The scene of Elijah and the prophets of Baal on Mount Carmel paints a profound picture on this point. Elijah and the prophets of Baal both agree to build up an altar and call upon the name of their respective deity to set a fire to their sacrifice. Whichever one answers by fire is God.

The prophets of Baal "called upon the name of Baal from morning till noon. . . . But there was no response; no one answered. . . . Midday passed, and . . . evening. . . . But there was no response, no one answered, no one paid attention" (1 Kings 18:26-29).

Then Elijah stepped forward, built up the altar, and prepared the sacrifice. He even requested that several large jars of water be poured upon the offering and on the altar. Then he prayed, "O LORD, God of Abraham, Isaac and Israel, let it be known today that you are God in Israel and that I am your servant. . . . Answer me, O LORD, answer me, so these people will know that you, O LORD, are God" (1 Kings 18:36-37).

The Lord answered Elijah's prayer with fire that burned the sacrifice and altar, and dried up all of the water that had been poured around the altar. All the people then knew that the Lord is God, and also, that this is the God who hears us and answers prayer.

God saves us. The word "salvation" denotes deliverance or liberation from sin. It is submission to God and the eternal divine plans and purposes. Having God as the source of deliverance, or salvation, mitigates one's fears. "The LORD is my light and my salvation—whom shall I fear? The LORD is the stronghold of my life—of whom shall I be afraid?" (Psalm 27:1).

To be in the kingdom of God is to have a radical value system based upon the life, death, and resurrection of Jesus of Nazareth. He alone is our salvation. "Salvation is found in no one else, for there is no other name under heaven given to men by which we must be saved" (Acts 4:12). We can conclude, then, that it is God's will that we be saved; it is God's will that we be delivered from sin.

God cares for us. It is a testimony of both faith and experience that God the Father cares for and provides for his children and his creation. It would be against the divine will for God to act in any other way. "Humble yourselves, therefore, under God's mighty hand, that he may lift you up in due time. Cast all your anxiety on him because he cares for you" (1 Peter 5:6-7).

God being for us (Romans 8:31) does not mean that our faith goes unchallenged. But the Bible and our own experiences give us confidence in God. What God has done not only gives us strength for today but also lays the groundwork for our future belief system. "Give thanks to the LORD, for he is good; his love endures forever. . . . They cried out to the LORD in their trouble, and he delivered them from their distress. . . . Let them give thanks to the LORD for his unfailing love and his wonderful deeds" (Psalm 107:1,6,8).

God gives promotions. God, with divine timing, places us where he wants us to be. In this world of clamoring for positions and power, we must understand promotions according to the value system demonstrated in the life of Jesus of Nazareth. Where and how far we go in life is determined by God's will for our lives and our submission to that will.

> God said to him, "No longer will you be called Abram; your name will be Abraham, for I have made you a father of many nations. I will make you very fruitful; I will make nations of you, and kings will come from you. I will establish my covenant as an everlasting covenant between me and you and your descendants after you. . . ." God also said to Abraham, "As for Sarai your wife, you are no longer to call her Sarai; her name will be Sarah. I will bless her and will surely give you a son by her. I will bless her so that she will be the mother of nations." (Genesis 17:5-7,15-16)

In these verses we see clearly God's will in promoting Sarah and Abraham. Because Sarai and Abram had done so well, God initiated a promotion of greater responsibility. A new position and greater salary are not promotions if they do not come from God. God is the only source of authentic promotions.

God disciplines us. To say that God disciplines the believer says, first of all, that God is a God of love. Second, it says that believers, no matter how great their faith, need to be disciplined. We are not yet where God wants us to be. So God, being a greater parent than our earthly parents, cannot stand by while we do as we please. "You are not your own;

you were bought at a price" (1 Corinthians 6:19b-20a). God the Father cannot allow his children to go without correction. There are degrees of discipline, and sometimes God's discipline is painful. But God disciplines us so that we might be molded into the very likeness of Jesus and that we might be all that God wants us to be in this life and in this world. That is the divine will for us. And as we understand more about the nature of God's discipline, we have a deeper insight into the will of God.

CHAPTER 2

A Biblical Analysis of God's Will

AN ANALYSIS OF CERTAIN CENTRAL PASSAGES IN THE BIBLE provides numerous opportunities for us to gain insight in interpreting the will of God. An excellent guide to such an analysis is Leslie Weatherhead's The Will of God, first published in 1944 and reprinted numerous times since then. A summation page at the front of one edition of that book states, "To understand the authentic will of God is to discover peace, to lose fear and confusion," and asserts that knowing the difference between God's will and our own self-deceptive counterfeit is "the beginning of wisdom, spiritual fulfillment and social purpose." Weatherhead divides God's will into three distinct types: intentional, circumstantial, and ultimate.

God's *intentional will* describes what God the Father wants for his children. God always wants what is best for us and is the only one who can determine what that is. God's intentional will can be frustrated only temporarily by humankind's free will. The interaction of our free will with God's intentional will is known as God's *circumstantial will*. A mystery surrounds this aspect of the divine will: we do not know why God allows certain things to happen that interfere with his supreme authority. However, by faith we know that God will not ultimately be defeated. What God intends may be slow in coming, but it will work out in the end. This end result is God's *ultimate* (or *final*) *will*.

To illustrate all of this, we may look at the game of football. When a quarterback goes back to pass the ball, the plan is to score a touchdown (intentional will). But there are defensive players who are out to prevent this quarterback from scoring (circumstantial will). In the end, the quarterback gets the ball in the end zone and the team scores the touchdown and wins the game (ultimate will).

An examination of some scriptural passages will help us to understand more clearly the nature of these three aspects of God's will.

The Will of God and Creation

In the creation narratives of Genesis 1–2, God's *intentional will* is that humankind live in a state of serenity with responsibilities. Having been made male and female in the image of God, humanity is given the garden, a place of serenity and uninterrupted fellowship with God. Yet within that garden, they are given dominion over God's creation with the charge of being stewards, or caretakers, of it. As long as they do not eat from the tree of the knowledge of good and evil, they maintain a state of innocence and live without fear of death.

We know from the Scriptures and from the reality of human existence that what God intended in creation is frustrated when the humans eat the fruit of the forbidden tree. In Genesis 3, God's *circumstantial will* allows Eve and her mate, Adam, to listen to the lies of the serpent and eat the fruit from the tree that gives knowledge of good and evil. From that point on, humanity is set on a course of life in rebellion against God. Not only conscious of our sins, we also are aware of our nakedness and must now attempt to cover up our transgressions as well as make excuses for our wrong choices. We are condemned to live in conflict with that over which we were given dominion, and our lives are filled with pain and with the anxiety of survival. After being expelled from Eden, our fellowship with God is now interrupted.

Yet even though humankind messed up badly, biblical faith declares that God, although momentarily frustrated, is never ultimately defeated. God's *ultimate will* prevails.

The apostle Paul makes this assertion of faith in his letter to the Roman church:

> I consider that our present sufferings are not worth comparing with the glory that will be revealed in us. The creation waits in eager expectation for the sons of God to be revealed. For the creation was subjected to frustration, not by its own choice, but by the will of the one who subjected it, in hope that the creation itself will be liberated from its bondage to decay and brought into the glorious freedom of the children of God. (Romans 8:18-21)

Paul is saying in this passage that God places a high premium on us that cannot be denied even when God's intentional will has been delayed. Adam and Eve can be made right with God. They can, once again, have unbroken fellowship with the Creator. Paul declares that nothing that God intends will ultimately be lost.

Paul gives another harbinger of hope that God's ultimate will finally overrides the failures that occurred because of God's circumstantial will. He says,

> And we know that in all things God works for the good of those who love him, who have been called according to his purpose. . . . Who shall separate us from the love of Christ? Shall trouble or hardship or persecution or famine or nakedness or danger or sword? . . . For I am convinced that neither death nor life, neither angels nor demons, neither the present nor the future, nor any powers, neither height nor depth, nor anything else in all creation,

will be able to separate us from the love of God that is in Christ Jesus our Lord. (Romans 8:28, 35, 38-39)

What God intends will surely come to pass. We must not become unglued because of the challenges presented by circumstances. God will have the last word, and creation will be rescued from chaos according to God's ultimate will.

The Will of God and the Election of Abraham and Israel

In analyzing the will of God in the Old Testament, it is essential that we deal with the election of a human being (Abraham) and a nation (Israel) to be a "light to the Gentiles." The Lord makes this promise to Abraham: "I will make you into a great nation and I will bless you; I will make your name great . . . and all peoples on earth will be blessed through you" (Genesis 12:2-3). Of the nation Israel, which eventually does come from the seed of Abraham and his wife, Sarah, the Lord says, "I will keep you and will make you to be a covenant for the people and a light for the Gentiles, to open eyes that are blind, to free captives from prison, and to release from the dungeon those who sit in darkness" (Isaiah 42:6b-7).

We see very clearly that Abraham and Israel were not chosen for privilege, but for responsibility. Therefore, Israel was no different from the other nations of the world at that time, except that it had a responsibility to bring those other nations into line with the will of God. In other words, Israel was elected to be an evangelist to the rest of the ancient world. Israel failed miserably when it began to feel superior to the rest of those nations. Israel's failure to grasp the significance of God's *intentional will* is what caused circumstances to arise that temporarily frustrated the intentional will of God. Israel survived many years without living up to what God had purposed for it. God was not defeated but was momentarily disappointed. God's next move was to give the light to his *ultimate will,* Jesus of Nazareth.

19

"When Jesus spoke again to the people, he said, 'I am the light of the world. Whoever follows me will never walk in darkness, but will have the light of life'" (John 8:12).

The Will of God and Joseph the Patriarch

In the Old Testament, the character of Joseph gives great insight into God's will. God's intentional will for Joseph's life is found in Genesis 37. There, Joseph had been tending sheep with his brothers and, upon returning home,

> he brought their father a bad report about them. Now [Jacob] loved Joseph more than any of his other sons, because he had been born to him in his old age; and he made a richly ornamented robe for him. When his brothers saw that their father loved him more than any of them, they hated him and could not speak a kind word to him. Joseph had a dream, and when he told it to his brothers, they hated him all the more. He said to them, . . . "We were binding sheaves of grain out in the field when suddenly my sheaf rose and stood upright, while your sheaves gathered around mine and bowed down to it." His brothers said to him, "Do you intend to reign over us? Will you actually rule us?" And they hated him all the more because of his dream and what he had said. Then he had another dream, and he told it to his brothers. . . . "This time, the sun and moon and eleven stars were bowing down to me." When he told his father as well as his brothers, his father rebuked him and said, "What is this dream you had? Will your mother and I and your brothers actually come and bow down to the ground before you?" His brothers were jealous of him; but his father kept the matter in mind. (Genesis 37:2-11)

In these verses, we can see clearly that God's *intentional will* was for Joseph to reign and rule. But several human issues emerged that frustrated the intentional will of God and created the circumstantial will of God: (1) Joseph informed his father of his brothers' bad behavior; (2) his father played the dangerous game of parental favoritism; (3) Joseph had dreams of greatness; and (4) his brothers were jealous of him because of the favoritism and because of the dreams.

Because of these factors, God's *circumstantial will* was set in place, and Joseph's brothers plotted to kill him (Genesis 37:18). In God's circumstantial will, the following events transpire that frustrate God's intentional will but serve as a prelude to God's ultimate or final will. In addition to the murder plot, two of his brothers (Reuben and Judah) keep him from getting killed; his brothers sell him into slavery; his father, Jacob, must live for years believing the lie told him by his other sons that his favorite child, Joseph, has been killed by a wild animal; and once Joseph is in Egypt, Joseph refuses the sexual advances of the wife of Potiphar, a powerful Egyptian official, and thereby ends up in prison (Genesis 37:19-34; 39:1-20).

Even though Joseph is in prison, God gives him the gift of interpreting dreams. With this gift, Joseph is set free after he interprets pharaoh's dream, and pharaoh puts him in charge of all of Egypt. God's *ultimate will* (the completion of intentional will) was for Joseph to be all that God had intended him to be. After many years of lying and deception on the part of Joseph's brothers, a great famine caused his family to come to Egypt to buy food. Though they did not recognize him immediately, Joseph knew them. In God's ultimate will, Joseph moved from the prison to the palace and was in a position to be the great person God intended him to be. Finally, he meets, greets, and forgives his brothers, and summons his father, Jacob, and the rest of his family to come to Egypt in order to survive.

> Then Joseph said to his brothers, "Come close to me. . . . I am your brother Joseph, the one you sold into Egypt! And now, do not be distressed and do not be angry with yourselves for selling me here, because it was to save lives that God sent me ahead of you. . . . God sent me ahead of you to preserve for you a remnant on earth and to save your lives by a great deliverance." (Genesis 45:4-5,7)

In the end, the family is together and reconciled. God's ultimate will was slow in coming, but it did come to pass.

The Will of God and the Issue of Slavery

The topic of slavery is full of complexities. Particularly in the community of the oppressed, nothing challenges inquiring minds like questions such as "Was it God's intentional will that European Americans enslave African Americans for three hundred years?" Nobody of sound mind would ever answer yes to that question. However, we must realize that it is humankind's alienation from God that makes some people feel superior or powerful enough to enslave other human beings.

Even though slavery existed in ancient Israel, slaves were to be treated fairly, and provisions in the law were made whereby slaves in various circumstances were set free. In Israel, unlike the United States, skin pigmentation was not the prime rationale for slavery. One could become a slave by hiring oneself out to a master, by being taken as a prisoner of war, or by owing a debt that one could not immediately pay. Slavery due to debt is the situation in the apostle Paul's letter to Philemon. In this very brief letter, Paul appeals on behalf of Onesimus, a runaway slave. Philemon is the legal owner of Onesimus, but Onesimus ran off without paying his debt to Philemon, and became a fugitive. Therefore, Paul says to Philemon,

> I appeal to you for my son Onesimus, who became my son while I was in chains. Formerly he was useless to you, but now he has become useful both to you and to me. I am sending him—who is my very heart—back to you. . . . Perhaps the reason he was separated from you for a little while was that you might have him back for good—no longer as a slave, but better than a slave, as a dear brother. . . . So if you consider me a partner, welcome him as you would welcome me. If he has done you any wrong or owes you anything, charge it to me. (Philemon 10–12,15–18)

Paul argues for brotherhood over and against one person's inhumanity against another. Because Paul steps in as Onesimus's liberator by offering to pay off his indebtedness to Philemon, Onesimus is no longer a slave. It is safe to say, then, that slavery has never been God's *intentional will*. Because of greed and obsession with skin pigmentation, however, slavery continues to be a reality in today's world. All slavery must be condemned. The community of faith must act as intercessor in the liberation of all peoples. Due to greed, prejudice, racism, and materialism, slavery has been tolerated in God's *circumstantial will*. However, the faith community lives in the hope of the transformation of history when all people will be brothers and sisters. That, then, will be the realization of God's *ultimate will*.

The Will of God and King Saul

One of the most tragic figures in biblical history is Saul, son of Kish. He is a classic example of a person who got caught in the crossfire between God's will and the will of the people. In 1 Samuel 8–31, we clearly see God's will on a collision course with that of the Israelites. God wanted the theocracy over Israel to continue (whereby God ruled through divinely anointed judges), but the people wanted a monarchy (rule by a king). God's *intentional will* was the continuation of a theocracy.

"When Samuel grew old, he appointed his sons as judges for Israel. . . . But his sons did not walk in his ways. They turned aside after dishonest gain and accepted bribes and perverted justice" (1 Samuel 8:1,3).

These two verses give us background and serve as a prelude to the request of the people for a king. Perhaps, if Samuel had been a better father, the people would have been satisfied with his sons as judges, and the theocracy would have continued. But such speculation does not surface in 1 Samuel 8, which records only the dissatisfaction and demand of the people that trigger the transition between the theocracy (time of the judges) and the monarchy in the history of Israel.

Because of the failure of Samuel's sons, the people now engage God's will in a negative way. We also see that the corrupt sons of Samuel are not the only reason that the people wanted a king.

> So all the elders of Israel gathered together and came to Samuel at Ramah. They said to him, "You are old, and your sons do not walk in your ways; now appoint a king to lead us, such as all the other nations have." But when they said, "Give us a king to lead us," this displeased Samuel; so he prayed to the LORD. And the LORD told him: "Listen to all that the people are saying to you; it is not you they have rejected, but they have rejected me. . . . Now listen to them; but warn them solemnly and let them know what the king who will reign over them will do." Samuel told all the words of the LORD to the people who were asking him for a king. . . . But the people refused to listen to Samuel. "No!" they said. "We want a king over us. Then we will be like all the other nations, with a king to lead us and to go out before us and fight our battles." When Samuel heard all that the people said, he repeated it before the LORD. The LORD answered, "Listen to them and give them a king." (1 Samuel 8:4-7,9-10,19-22a)

Therefore, it is apparent that God's *intentional will* is for Israel not to have a king. However, the people ignore Samuel and request a king, and under the *circumstantial will* of God, the will of the people will prevail for almost five hundred years.

Saul is selected and anointed as king (1 Samuel 9–11). In all of this, Saul seems not to care one way or another. He goes out in search of his father's donkeys, and when he returns, he is chief candidate for king. Even though Saul was anointed king by Samuel under God's circumstantial will, he still could have been blessed had he obeyed God. What would have happened if Saul had refused to be king? We must remember that although Saul was caught between God's will and the will of the people, he still could have exercised his free will and refused to be king. Tending donkeys is far better than being a king who is reigning against God's will. The fact that God does not end the monarchy with Saul is evidence of divine mercy even when we are out of God's intentional will (1 Samuel 16).

Ultimately, Saul is rejected and destroyed not because he is king, even though his kingship is against the intentional will of God. He is rejected because he fails to obey God (1 Samuel 15). This can be clearly seen, especially in the life of David, who was called "a man after [God's] own heart" (1 Samuel 13:14). And, even though Saul is killed on Mount Gilboa, the monarchy, as we noted earlier, lasts for another five hundred years. The monarchy ends with Zedekiah, who is carried into captivity by the Babylonians (Jeremiah 39:5-7).

God's intentional will is partially fulfilled when the monarchy effectively ends in 586 B.C.E. with the Babylonian exile. (In the second and first centuries B.C.E., the Hasmonean dynasty ruled after the Maccabean Revolt, but even that resurrection of Judaic monarchy did not endure.) In New Testament times, Herod the Great bore the title of king, but he was simply a puppet of the Roman Empire (Matthew 2:1-3). But although the monarchy is no more, the theocracy that God wanted is not yet. It still lies in the future.

"The seventh angel sounded his trumpet, and there were loud voices in heaven, which said: 'The kingdom of the world has become the kingdom of our Lord and of his Christ, and he will reign for ever and ever'" (Revelation 11:15).

The Will of God and Judas Iscariot

The selection of Judas Iscariot to be a disciple appears to be an amazing paradox, especially since it comes as a result of Jesus praying all night (Luke 6:12-16). Think of it: Jesus prays all night and still chooses Judas! This should be a lesson to us that prayer does not exempt us from misfortune. The selection of Judas raises the question of why God chooses any of us. Every one of us is capable of being a Judas Iscariot. Only by taking the high road of commitment to Christ can we escape betrayal. That which was in Judas is in all of us; but in his case, what was in him got the better of him, and he acted out publicly on it.

Some take the "Calvinistic" position that Judas was predestined to betray Jesus. But, if that is true, how could Judas be guilty? Jesus replied,

> "The Son of Man will go just as it is written about him. But woe to that man who betrays the Son of Man! It would be better for him if he had not been born." Then Judas, the one who would betray him, said, "Surely not I, Rabbi?" Jesus answered, "Yes, it is you." (Matthew 26:23-25)

This seems to indicate that Judas, although he is a part of the greatest drama in human history, was not bereft of the freedom to choose to do good. If this is just high-class drama, then Judas deserved an Academy Award for best actor, and Jesus should have received one for best producer for pulling together the whole dreadful ordeal. But what is God's will in all of this?

God's *intentional will* is for Judas to trust and obey, no matter what temptations engage him. Imagine what a powerful witness he was until he betrayed his Lord. Judas is not chosen so that Jesus will have someone to betray him; rather, he is chosen to be a charter member of a movement that both transforms and transcends history. But Judas blows it. He blows it with his eyes wide open (John 13:27). Even though, as John 13:27 notes, Satan entered him, this is no excuse. Satan can possess only those who are leaning away from Christ. Judas was not a poor, pitiful, or helpless man. He had the freedom to choose for Christ rather than against him.

In regard to God's *circumstantial will*, we must raise the question of why Judas followed Jesus in the first place. At the outset, he may have been sincere. When he attempts to manipulate divine providence, however, he is doomed to defeat. It is not the thirty pieces of silver that gets to him, but rather his desire to force Jesus to become the militaristic messiah that he and the others think Jesus should be. Judas wants to defeat the Roman occupation of Palestine; perhaps the Roman power will be wiped out by the angelic host (Matthew

26:53). But when Jesus fails to be the messiah according to Judas, Judas returns the money and hangs himself (Matthew 27:1-5). Instead of remaining loyal to Jesus, Judas overplays his hand, and as a result, Jesus is crucified.

In spite of Judas's defection, Jesus is not ultimately defeated. God's *ultimate will*—that Christ emerge, resurrected and victorious over death—is achieved through a cross.

The Meaning of "Your Will Be Done on Earth As It Is in Heaven" (Matthew 6:10)

As we seek to know God, we must try to act like God in this world. Only then is God's will "done on earth as it is in heaven." Matthew 6:10 carries a reminder that we are not exempt from earthly defeat, disaster, depression, or disease. God permits things to happen that are contrary to his intentional will. It is not God's *intentional will* that some of our emergency blood supply be tainted with the AIDS virus. God's *circumstantial will*, however, tells us that we live in a world where this disease does occur and where some people who donate their blood are infected with this virus. However, as we see it now, God's *ultimate will* appears to be that even though the disease is still with us, the emergency blood supply, through proper screening and testing, can be protected and used for our good.

"Your will be done on earth as it is in heaven" assures us that there are some things that God will not ask us to do. Many a maniac has believed that he or she understands God's will. The young man who killed Martin Luther King Jr.'s mother, Alberta King, believed that God had directed him to do what he did. Yet we know for certain that God would not have directed this man to perform such a deed.

God's will can be painful, and sometimes we will question it here on earth. In spite of knowing what we know about God from Scripture and experience, some things will occur that we will not understand. A classic example is God's servant Job, whose problem ran deeper than the loss of his family and material goods. His problem went all the way to his deficient theology. He saw God's will for the righteous as all sunshine and no rain. We know that is not the case. Matthew 6:10 in its most basic interpretation means that even though God is sovereign and rules by righteous love, this earth is not yet paradise—not even for the righteous. And, on our way to paradise, we must negotiate the ambiguities of life on this planet. We must live our lives according to the dictates of God and, ultimately, all earthly kingdoms must yield to God's kingdom.

The Meaning of Gethsemane (Matthew 26:36-46)

First and foremost, Gethsemane tells us that we can discover God's will through prayer.

> Then Jesus went with his disciples to a place called Gethsemane, and he said to them, "Sit here while I go over there and pray." . . . Going a little farther, he fell with his face to the ground and prayed, "My Father, if it is possible, may this cup be taken from me. Yet not as I will, but as you will." . . . He went away a second time and prayed, "My Father, if it is not possible for this cup to be taken away unless I drink it, may your will be done." . . . So he left them and went away once more and prayed the third time, saying the same thing. (Matthew 26:36,39,42,44)

Gethsemane also means that our will is often in conflict with God's will. It means that Jesus, like us, faced doubts, disappointments, and defeats. But the cup—the struggle—was deeper than this. The cup was about the Son of God becoming sin, with all of its depravity (2 Corinthians 5:21). The struggle involved Jesus going from absolute perfection to abject sinfulness!

The phrase "Yet not as I will, but as you will" is the bridge that takes us from our will to God's will. Gethsemane means that once we understand God's will, we must surrender. Only then can we experience real peace while the will of God prevails. (This is discussed further in chapter 3.)

The Will of God and the Cross

Many Christians believe that Jesus came into the world to die, in part because the Gospels, which were written thirty years after the crucifixion, with a retrospective understanding of Jesus' life and death, looked upon the cross as the will of God (see Mark 10:45). Even a casual perusal of Scripture as a whole reveals that this is not the case at all. If the sole purpose for Christ's birth was his atoning death, then he could have died as an infant, in the slaughter of the innocents under Herod the Great. Jesus came to call Israel, which was chosen to be the light to the rest of the world (Isaiah 42:6), to repentance.

"These twelve Jesus sent out with the following instructions: 'Do not go among the Gentiles or enter any town of the Samaritans. Go rather to the lost sheep of Israel'" (Matthew 10:5-6).

Therefore, the cross is not immediately God's *intentional will;* it is God's *circumstantial will.* Weatherhead reasons this way:

> Was it God's intention from the beginning that Jesus should go to the Cross? I think the answer to that question must be No. . . . He came with the *intention* that men should follow him, not kill him. . . . The discipleship of men, not the death of Christ, was the intentional will of God. . . . But when circumstances wrought by men's evil set up such a dilemma that Christ was compelled either to die or to run away, then *in those circumstances* the Cross was the will of God. . . . So, in regard to the Cross, God achieved his final goal not simply in spite of the Cross, but through it. (*The Will of God,* pp. 12–13)

Even though the cross is a painful reality created by sin, God's *ultimate will* is achieved through the resurrection. The resurrection becomes the means by which humanity claims Christ's victory over sin, and through that victory, we are reconciled to God.

CHAPTER 3

Jesus of Nazareth

TO KNOW JESUS OF NAZARETH IS TO KNOW THE WILL OF GOD. The biblical Jesus is the ultimate image of God. He is the incarnation, embodiment of God; he gives God a face. The Gospel of John gives profound expression of this great mystery—God in the flesh—that stands at the center of the Christian faith.

> In the beginning was the Word, and the Word was with God, and the Word was God. He was with God in the beginning. Through him all things were made; without him nothing was made that has been made. In him was life, and that life was the light of men. The light shines in the darkness, but the darkness has not understood it. . . . The Word became flesh and made his dwelling among us. We have seen his glory, the glory of the One and Only, who came from the Father, full of grace and truth. (John 1:1-5,14)

Light can be seen in other religions, but Christians believe that God's supreme self-revelation is seen in Jesus of Nazareth. The Word, which is the preexistent will of God, became visible in him. If we agree that Jesus of Nazareth was God in the flesh, we must conclude that what he says and does is of ultimate concern. Since God is with us in the person of Jesus, the divine will pervades the realm of our daily lives. Therefore, Jesus' attitude on issues determines the stances that we, as Christians, must take. When we fail to consider Jesus, the incarnation of God, then inevitably we will be confused about the will of God in our lives and in this world.

The Early Years of Jesus

We cannot come to a basic understanding of God's will unless we look at the beginning of Jesus' earthly life. Although we do not know a great deal about Jesus' early years, there are some insights to be gained from what we do know.

> So Joseph also went up from the town of Nazareth in Galilee to Judea, to Bethlehem the town of David, because he belonged to the house and line of David. He went there to register with Mary, who was pledged to be married to him and was expecting a child. While they were there, the time came for the baby to be born, and she gave birth to her firstborn, a son. She wrapped him in cloths and placed him in a manger, because there was no room for them in the inn. (Luke 2:4-7)

What does this have to do with the will of God? The birth of Jesus in a stable declares that the circumstances of one's birth do not have to doom one to a life of defeat. The fact that an individual is born in a lowly situation does not necessarily mean that he or she cannot soar to great heights. Was it God's intentional will that Jesus be born in an animal stall, or was this the circumstantial will of God? Should he have been born in a palace? Since God, in Christ, showed up in the barn, it cannot be dismissed as insignificant. The message of the barn is that, in reality, the palace can be a serious impediment to the mission of the kingdom.

Beyond this, we must not shy away from the fact that it appears to be God's will that Jesus be born in a small town (Bethlehem) and also grow up in one (Nazareth). People from all walks of life have struggled with the stigma of having grown up in a "hick town." In our culture of "mega" this and "ultra" that, we feel very uncomfortable when a job transfer sends us to the equivalent of a Bethlehem or a

Nazareth. Many a preacher feels compelled to find a church in Los Angeles, Atlanta, Dallas, or some other large metropolitan center. But the question is this: Can God's will be discovered in obscurity? Jesus answers that question in the affirmative. God can fulfill the divine will for our lives no matter where we are.

Similarly, the fact that Jesus was a carpenter is not an impediment to establishing God's will. God is so unlike us! If the choice were ours, we most likely would have made Jesus a professor of philosophy, a medical doctor, or a multibillionaire. But it was God's will that Jesus' vocation be that of a carpenter. No wonder we stumble over God even while we are looking for him: the biblical Jesus constantly violates the rules of our class boundaries. While we often think that we will find the divine will in suburbia, we are shocked when we discover that God is equally at home in the life of an inner-city hotel employee or mill worker. It was God's intentional will for Jesus to be a carpenter.

Looking to Jesus' formative years, we see that his appearance in the temple at the age of twelve is essential for understanding God's will. Jesus had accompanied his parents on their annual journey to Jerusalem to celebrate the Passover. On the way home, thinking that Jesus was with the group, his parents traveled for a full day before noticing his absence and beginning to look for him. Unable to find him, they immediately returned to Jerusalem. There, they frantically searched for him for three days before finding him in the temple, sitting among the rabbis.

> [Jesus was] listening to them and asking them questions. Everyone who heard him was amazed at his understanding and his answers. When his parents saw him, they were astonished. His mother said to him, "Son, why have you treated us like this? Your father and I have been anxiously searching for you." "Why were you searching for me?" he asked. "Didn't you know I had to be in my Father's house?" But they did not understand what he was saying to them. Then he went down to Nazareth with them and was obedient to them. (Luke 2:46-51)

This passage points out the tension that exists between being loyal both to God and to God-ordained institutions. How can one be in God's will when other legitimate structures such as families and governments are beckoning? It can become difficult to draw the line, and sometimes chaos ensues.

When Jesus is found in the temple, there is a conflict between his family's will and God's will for his life. This dilemma has far-reaching implications, leading all the way to Jesus' resurrection. Within the temple scene, we can discern God's *intentional will* for Jesus. God intends for Jesus (1) to learn about his faith and culture; (2) to put God's will first; (3) to begin his quest for learning; (4) to have caring parents; and (5) to obey God and his parents.

It was God's *circumstantial will* that this conflict would occur during other times in Jesus' life. In one such time, Jesus is teaching the crowds when his mother and brothers try to see him, but to no avail. And in one of the most heart-wrenching scenes of the Bible, Jesus is hanging on the cross as his mother looks on hopelessly. It required much prayer, faith, and wisdom for Jesus to negotiate through those difficult times. But, as we see in Acts 1:14, it was God's *ultimate will* that his family would come to believe in him after his resurrection.

Other conflicts can occur between God's will for our lives and the requirements placed upon us by the governing authorities. The apostle Paul's analysis of this conflict helps us to discover God's will when a Christian confronts the government.

> Therefore, it is necessary to submit to the authorities, not only because of possible punishment but also because of conscience. This is why you pay taxes, for the authorities are God's servants, who give their full time to governing. Give everyone what you owe him: If you owe taxes, pay taxes; if revenue, then revenue; if respect, then respect; if honor, then honor. (Romans 13:5-7)

The foundation of Paul's ethic is based on Jesus' analysis of this challenge to know God's will. Jesus answered the Pharisees, "Give to Caesar what is Caesar's, and to God what is

God's" (Matthew 22:21). It is a continuing struggle to know God's will in this matter because governments are invariably unjust and our leaders often lack integrity. What, then, is the will of God? The question is answered by the deaths of Jesus and Paul, both under the authority of the Roman government. Jesus offered the kingdom of God as the ultimate statement that we must protest unjust structures. Whenever government is in conflict with the kingdom of Jesus, we must be loyal to him, even to the point of suffering and death.

The Temptations of Jesus

The temptations of Jesus also provide special insight into God's will for our lives.

> Then Jesus was led by the Spirit into the desert to be tempted by the devil. After fasting forty days and forty nights, he was hungry. The tempter came to him and said, "If you are the Son of God, tell these stones to become bread." Jesus answered, "It is written: 'Man does not live on bread alone, but on every word that comes from the mouth of God.'" (Matthew 4:1-4)

This first temptation shows that it is God's will that there be a balance between the physical and the spiritual. The battle between the hunger of the stomach and the hunger of the soul is ongoing. It is God's will for the total self to be fed. While miracles are an intrinsic part of the New Testament faith, Jesus never used the miraculous as an attempt to cancel reality. Saved people need bread, but they are not saved by bread. While bread helps us to maintain a healthy existence, we are saved by the Bread of Life, who is the Word of God. While we need both, we must not confuse the two.

In the second temptation, the devil taunts Jesus to jump from "the highest point of the temple" to see if God's angels will catch him. Jesus replies, "Do not put the Lord Your God to the test" (Matthew 4:5-7).

In this temptation, Jesus refuses to be a sanctified stunt-man. It is God's will for us that we "live by faith, and not by sight" (2 Corinthians 5:7). The kingdom of God is not established by levitation or other crafts of the magician. Sensationalism is beneficial in boosting the ratings of television news broadcasts, but is not edifying for the kingdom of God. Many Christian "mega" ministries are successful as a result of using sensational tactics. Their philosophy is "Get them in at any cost." Jesus' philosophy is "Get them in by letting them count the cost."

For the final temptation, the devil offers Jesus all the kingdoms and riches of the world if he will only bow down and worship him. Jesus asserts his supreme authority by telling the devil, "Away from me, Satan! For it is written: 'Worship the Lord your God, and serve him only'" (Matthew 4:10).

This temptation points out the danger of power. We can be powerful and successful, but at what price? We must always consider the source of our power or success. God's *intentional will* was for Jesus to establish the kingdom without taking a shortcut. God's *circumstantial will* was temptation, rejection, and the cross. Any success that evades "the way of the cross" is bankrupt and superficial. God's *ultimate will* will be established in the end time. Jesus defeated Satan because he refused to take the world's path to glory. For him, the way of the cross led to victory.

The Teachings of Jesus

One of the ways that we can discern the will of God is by looking at what Jesus said. His word is of the greatest value. When he speaks, Christians listen! His teachings on the will of God can be summarized by a review of what he said in the Beatitudes (Matthew 5:1-12), the Sermon on the Mount (Matthew 5-7), and some of his parables. In addition, although the popular question "What would Jesus do?" appears so often on Christian novelty items, it actually is an essential question that must be answered by people of faith who are seriously seeking to know the will of God in their lives.

According to the Beatitudes, it is God's will that we

- exemplify humility
- have a repentant spirit
- be nonaggressive in our relationships with others
- have an insatiable appetite for the things of God
- be models of mercy
- not allow our vision of Jesus to be obstructed by the things of the world
- be drum majors for peace and justice
- be willing to suffer verbal and physical abuse for the cause of Christ

In other words, our lives must change drastically. When our lives exemplify God's will, no one can doubt who it is we live for. But there's more.

According to the Sermon on the Mount, the will of God tells us we must not only control our anger, but also we must put a moratorium on revenge, practice forgiveness, and actually love our enemies while taking the initiative toward reconciliation. We not only control our lusts, but also we take our marriage vows seriously. We practice honesty in all relationships and tell the truth in love. Yes, we fast and pray, but we are called to be authentic disciples without making a public display of our faith in order to receive the approval of the "religious" crowd. We trust that God, our Father, will take care of his children, yet we develop a spirit of discernment in order to distinguish between that which is of God and that which is false. To accomplish all of this, we build our lives upon the firm foundation: our faith in Jesus of Nazareth.

Beyond the Sermon on the Mount, the Gospels and the Epistles give further expression of the transformative teaching of Jesus. While the Sermon on the Mount is the core of his teaching, everything that Jesus said, especially the parables, gives insight into the will of God.

In Matthew 13:3-8, Jesus tells a parable commonly known as the parable of the sower, but which is more aptly called the parable of the soils.

A farmer went out to sow his seed. As he was scattering the seed, some fell along the path, and the birds came and ate it up. Some fell on rocky places, where it did not have much soil. It sprang up quickly, because the soil was shallow. But when the sun came up, the plants were scorched, and they withered because they had no root. Other seed fell among thorns, which grew up and choked the plants. Still other seed fell on good soil, where it produced a crop—a hundred, sixty or thirty times what was sown.

Jesus gives a fuller explanation of this parable in Matthew 13:18-23. However, the parable by itself pulsates with profound gems of wisdom as it highlights the will of God. This parable makes it clear that it is the divine will that God's Word be delivered everywhere. Although people are free to reject as well as to receive the Word of God, those who freely receive the Word will be rewarded. It is God's *intentional will* that all receive and remain in the Word. But because of the freedom to reject God's intentional will, God's *circumstantial will* kicks in and there will be a substantial failure rate. However, God's *ultimate will* prevails and some will remain in the Word. This is God's final will.

In Matthew 13:24-30, Jesus tells the crowd the parable of the wheat and the tares. In this parable, an enemy comes into a farmer's field at night and sows weeds among the wheat. As the wheat grows, so do the weeds. The farmer instructs the servants to let the weeds grow among the wheat until harvest time, when the two will be separated.

This parable, where the weeds represent evil, teaches us that it is God's will that we deal with the reality of evil. Further light is shed on the will of God when we understand the human factor in evil. In v. 25 Jesus says, *"But while everyone was sleeping,* his enemy came" (emphasis added). This shows us that sometimes an evil can be explained by the failure of humankind to act or speak out against it. Yet, although the servants slept, there is no evidence that the farmer was asleep. "Indeed, he who watches over Israel will neither slumber nor sleep" (Psalm 121:4). It is clear, and we must understand, that God is the source of good and yet still permits evil. Therefore, we must be discerning and patient with this discomforting fellowship between good and evil.

God, who is represented by the farmer, is a paragon of wisdom. And wisdom is a great virtue to possess as we deal with evil in the world. Still, why does God permit this evil to occur? This is a question that, by faith, we answer by declaring that God has it all under control. While God's *intentional will* was that the wheat exist alone in the field, God's *circumstantial will* allowed for the weeds, which came about because of human freedom. Freedom is a gift from God, but it can be used against God's intentional will. But, God's *ultimate will* will be accomplished in the harvest. Evil cannot survive the ultimate scrutiny of judgment.

The parables of the lost sheep, the lost coin, and the lost son (Luke 15) also give insight into the will of God. In this trilogy, we clearly see where the heart of God is. And in all three parables, the will of God is established. In all three parables

- to be lost is the antithesis of God's intentional will
- the importance of the individual is emphasized ("the very hairs of your head are all numbered" [Luke 12:7])
- God's love is manifested
- God's will for humankind is community: the one is returned to the many

The Actions of Jesus

To determine the will of God through the question "What would Jesus do?" we may look at the Gospels to determine "What *did* Jesus do?" First, Jesus healed the sick (Luke 8:40-56). The healing ministry of Jesus is a declaration of God's *intentional* and *ultimate wills.* Sickness is God's *circumstantial will,* because we live in a world that is not yet redeemed.

Jesus cleansed lepers (Luke 7:22). Leprosy was not only a devastating physical malady but was also an odious social stigma. A leper was an untouchable. But the ministry of Jesus declares that it is God's will for Christians to bring healing to life's untouchables.

Jesus cast out devils (Luke 8:26-39). Jesus' ministry of exorcism is a declaration that God's will for us is to be free from any malevolent spirit that causes us to be alienated from God, people, and the environment.

Jesus raised the dead (Luke 7:11-17). These restorations to life were not permanent; they were an interruption of the inevitable. Death is a reality. However, these restorations are a token of God's will. They declare that God's *intentional will* is that we not experience death or the anxiety that surrounds it. But because we live in a world that has not been finally reconciled to God, death will continue to be both friend and foe. Death is a reality because of God's *circumstantial will.* But because of the restorations that are a prelude to the resurrection of Jesus of Nazareth, God's *ultimate will* will be established with our own resurrection. "The body that is sown is perishable, it is raised imperishable; it is sown in dishonor, it is raised in glory; it is sown in weakness, it is raised in power; it is sown a natural body, it is raised a spiritual body" (1 Corinthians 15:42b-44).

Jesus and Gethsemane

An examination of the garden of Gethsemane is pivotal in any discussion of the will of God. In the garden of Eden, we see the beginning of our alienation from God, humankind, ourselves, and the environment (Genesis 3). In Gethsemane, we find that the process for the reconciliation of all things is beginning to take shape through Jesus discerning and submitting to God's will.

> Then Jesus went with his disciples to a place called Gethsemane, and he said to them, "Sit here while I go over there and pray." . . . Going a little farther, he fell with his face to the ground and

> prayed, "My Father, if it is possible, may this cup be taken from me. Yet not as I will, but as you will." . . . He went away a second time and prayed, "My Father, if it is not possible for this cup to be taken away unless I drink it, may your will be done." . . . So he left them and went away once more and prayed the third time, saying the same thing. (Matthew 26:36,39,42,44)

Gethsemane is the place in our pilgrimage as disciples of Jesus where we must bridge the gulf that separates our will from God's. Gethsemane is not about deciding which house to buy or choosing whom to marry. It is about making a choice between death and desertion. This is the "big leagues" of decision-making. Once we get there, we are in another zone. German theologian Dietrich Bonhoeffer (1906–45), who was martyred by Hitler's Nazi government, and Martin Luther King Jr. (1929–68) both made such a choice. Bonhoeffer left the relative security of America to return to Germany and to face death as a protester of Hitler's evil government. Martin Luther King Jr. made the choice to leave the comfort of Atlanta to return to Memphis, where he was assassinated on April 4, 1968. This kind of decision-making is foreign to our prosperity- and success-oriented American Christianity.

Gethsemane is not about praise and worship; it is about accepting God's will even if we must die. The decision of whether to die or to desert is voluntary. However, it is a decision that makes us a victor, a victim, or a coward. It is the great division between death, defeat, desertion, defilement, and destiny.

For Jesus, the "cup" of Gethsemane was his identification as sin. In other words, he was saying to God, "Is redemption possible without my being defiled as sin?" Scripture says of Jesus, "God made him who had no sin to be sin for us, so that in him we might become the righteousness of God" (2 Corinthians 5:21). Jesus, then, makes the decision to die in order that we might live.

Jesus also said to his disciples, "If anyone would come after me, he must deny himself and take up his cross and follow me. For whoever wants to save his life will lose it, but whoever loses his life for me will find it" (Matthew 16:24-25). To make the decision to die is the essence of discipleship. Bonhoeffer, in *The Cost of Discipleship,* said, "When Jesus calls a person, he bids him to come and die." This is the call of Gethsemane.

The path that Jesus took in negotiating the challenge of Gethsemane may be described as follows: He believed in the power and efficacy of prayer. For him, prayer was not psychological projection. It was the medium through which we discover and accept the divine will. In the life of Jesus, prayer was not about getting our own way; it was about God having his way. Jesus also believed in the power of persistent prayer. He knew that often it takes time to discover God's will in our lives. Jesus believed in human freedom, knowing that freedom is not doing as we please but doing as we should. He accepted the reality of the situation and submitted to the sovereignty of God.

Sometimes the answer to the perplexity of pain is to embrace it and engage it, and by doing so, to find God's will. The issue in Gethsemane is not God's *intentional will,* for it has been established from all eternity that we would come to know God through his Incarnate One, Jesus. Jesus' imminent betrayal is God's *circumstantial will.* Because of human freedom, Jesus finds himself agreeing with the Father to take the way of the cross. Once he does, God's *ultimate will* is made known through the pain of Good Friday and the peace of Resurrection Sunday.

Jesus and the Cross

The cross is at the center of authentic Christianity. In an ultimate sense, the cross is not a piece of wood; it is a bleeding carpenter. There is no salvation in a piece of wood. Salvation is in Jesus of Nazareth. He is the cross. The cross is the ultimate arbiter of pain and purpose. It is both purposeful and perplexing. Once Jesus passed the test of seeking God's will in Gethsemane, he voluntarily lined up with the will of

God—death by crucifixion. By his own volition, he chose to die by crucifixion rather than to live for even one second out of the Father's will. At any moment, he could have called the whole thing off. He could have apologized to the religious establishment and lived to a ripe old age. But he had crossed the line that separated time from eternity. Either he was crazy or he was the Christ! He could not deny his sonship, and thus he chose death rather than denial.

The cross is amazing because the Incarnate One dies in our place. This notion of "substitutionary atonement" is a major tenet of Christian theology. Christ carries out the will of God and dies in our place. The *intentional will* of God was that humankind accept Jesus as Lord and that the nation of Israel repent and accept the Messiah. However, Christ was rejected. That rejection became God's *circumstantial will,* which led to the crucifixion. The cross, as it expresses the circumstantial will of God, is about powerlessness. Both the Roman Empire and the Jewish religious empire were seemingly too much to overcome. What can we do when the religious/political establishment is stacked against us? How can we win?

Therein lies the victory. The cross as the circumstantial will of God is about feeling as if we are being forsaken by God. Even though we know that God will never leave us or forsake us (Hebrews 13:5), when a person, James Byrd, is dragged to his death while tied to a speeding pickup truck in Texas at the close of the twentieth century, it is hard to believe that there are never times when we are forsaken by God. Jesus, the Son of God, who became sin, knew all too well the painful depths of feeling forsaken.

"From the sixth hour until the ninth hour darkness came over all the land. About the ninth hour Jesus cried out in a loud voice, 'Eloi, Eloi, lama sabachthani?'—which means, 'My God, my God, why have you forsaken me?'" (Matthew 27:45-46).

Even though the cross is pain personified, Jesus refused to let his pain paralyze him and keep him from accomplishing his God-ordained purpose. In his pain on the cross, he saved one repenting sinner, and he refused to be dismayed at being rejected by a second sinner. Miraculously and mysteriously, he went through the "valley of the shadow" experiencing our pain because it was his very own.

The will of God as expressed through the cross forces us to trust God. It is like driving through a tunnel where no u-turns are allowed. We must keep on driving, because we know that there is light at the end of the tunnel. Therefore, it is God's will that in the midst of our pain we must trust God either to transform our pain or to give us the grace to see the divine purposes come to fruition.

In spite of, and also because of, the pain, God's love was at its best at the cross. While it was dark, the light shone most brightly. The cross removes the aura of cheap sentimentality and makes us confront love at its deepest level. "For God so loved the world that he gave his one and only Son, that whoever believes in him shall not perish but have eternal life" (John 3:16). We cannot know that love (in Greek: *agape*) until we submit ourselves to the painful reality of being obedient to the will of God.

God can accomplish great miracles when we choose the divine will above our own. The greatest miracle is not feeling no pain, but rather it is allowing God to transform our pain into paradise. On October 3, 1992, in the closing minutes of a football game between Florida State University and the University of Miami, Miami's great quarterback and Heisman Trophy winner Gino Torretta faded back and threw a long touchdown pass to the equally great receiver Lamar Thomas, as Miami came from behind to beat Florida State. Even though there was celebration in the end zone, Gino Torretta had been hit by a blitzing linebacker, and he lay on the ground, writhing in pain. Victory romped in the end zone, but pain was lying on the playing field. Would the quarterback get up? That was the question. When Jesus died on the cross, the victory was assured, but the question remained: "Will he get up?"

Jesus and the Resurrection

The foregoing question was answered in the resurrection of Jesus. Therefore, God's final will was expressed. The resurrection is God's declaration that triumph can come out of suffering. The arc of the moral universe bends toward life rather than death. (By the way, Gino Torretta did get up! And that great receiver, Lamar Thomas, is my nephew!)

The resurrection did not reverse the pain of the cross; it transformed it. It does not say that the cross was a mistake; it says that in light of God's *intentional will,* there was no other option that would have been satisfying to God. The cross was necessary so that God could establish his final will through the resurrection. There is no resurrection unless we die. And the pain of death is the prelude to the resurrection; the resurrection, then, takes the pain out of death.

"Where, O death, is your victory? Where, O death, is your sting?" (1 Corinthians 15:55).

As a result, the resurrection has launched the church as the body of Christ, unleashed the ministry of the Holy Spirit for its empowerment, and has given us the New Testament as the guide for its faith and practice. Because the resurrection is about overcoming and standing above our circumstances, God's *ultimate will* will be realized with the redemption of all things under the lordship of Jesus of Nazareth.

CHAPTER 4

Suffering

A MYSTERY OF THE JUDEO-CHRISTIAN FAITH IS THAT IT WOULD dare to claim that God's will is often made known through suffering. This reality is at the heart of the Christian faith. The age in which we live tries to evade this enigma, but we must face it. Furthermore, our reaction to suffering can be a tremendous impediment to a clear understanding of God's will. When we suffer, depending upon the degree to which we suffer, we tend to feel abandoned by God. But we will forever be bereft of spiritual vision until we can see God in both the sunshine and the rain. God is the Lord of both.

Redemptive Suffering

Anyone who looks at the cross and fails to see God's will in operation there will never understand the divine will. The cross is the great medium for understanding God's will. God's will was never more apparent than in the suffering of Jesus of Nazareth.

> When they came to the place called the Skull, there they crucified him, along with the criminals—one on his right, the other on his

left. . . . It was now about the sixth hour, and darkness came over the whole land until the ninth hour, for the sun stopped shining. And the curtain of the temple was torn in two. Jesus called out with a loud voice, "Father, into your hands I commit my spirit." (Luke 23:33,44-46a)

The casual observer of Calvary would conclude that this was a great tragedy involving a good but deluded prophet who was rubbed out by the religious/political establishment. Yet in spite of this, we declare the suffering of Jesus to be "redemptive." What is redemptive suffering? It is voluntary suffering that wipes out the individual but saves the community. It is meritorious, not because of the injury done to the individual, but because of the blessings that are bequeathed to the group. This is not fatalism. It is, rather, the genius of God in transforming suffering into salvation. The life of Martin Luther King Jr. (1929–68), to a lesser degree, was also redemptive in that an individual died for the community. In death, he accomplished far more than he did in his life. Yet his sacrificial life gave meaning to his death.

The suffering of Jesus of Nazareth is central to the notion of faith in authentic Christianity. God was present in a dying carpenter on a skull-shaped hill on a blood-soaked cross. But did Jesus come in order to get killed? Was it God's will for him to suffer such a horrible death? If so, then would we need to applaud Herod the Great for his attempt upon the life of the young child Jesus? As we look back at the cross, we can see that the suffering of Jesus was in the will of God, but as stated in chapter 2, it is insufficient theology to say that he came solely (or even primarily) to die. He did not come to die. Initially, he came to call Israel to repentance (Matthew 15:24). But when he was rejected, he willingly accepted crucifixion as a panacea for Jewish *and* Gentile salvation. Therefore, we conclude that God's *intentional will* was for the Jewish people to be the "light" of redemption for the whole world.

When Jesus came and was rejected by the religious establishment of his day, the *circumstantial will* of God was the cross. The voluntary death of Jesus then became the medium of liberation for the whole world. In spite of the crucifixion of Jesus, God's *ultimate will* has been established, is being established, and will yet be established. This has been done through the resurrection, Pentecost, the ministry of the Holy Spirit through the church, the inspiration of the New Testament, and the return of Jesus to be King of kings and Lord of lords. Because of this, millions upon millions have claimed him as Lord.

Suffering for the Sake of Righteousness

Christians are not exempt from suffering. There is a direct connection between our suffering and our commitment to Christ.

> Dear friends, do not be surprised at the painful trial you are suffering, as though something strange were happening to you. But rejoice that you participate in the sufferings of Christ, so that you may be overjoyed when his glory is revealed. . . . So then, those who suffer according to God's will should commit themselves to their faithful Creator and continue to do good. (1 Peter 4:12-13,19)

This is foreign to most Christians in the United States because we live in a materialistic culture that substitutes the American Christ for the biblical Christ. No wonder we have created strange theologies! In many instances, we are preaching what the apostle Paul calls "another gospel—which is no gospel at all" (Galatians 1:6-7). It needs to be said that God is not a sadist. God gets no pleasure out of seeing us suffer, but God does receive glory when we suffer gladly.

It is not God's *intentional will* that we suffer, but rather that we so commit ourselves to God that our lives become a powerful witness. However, the *circumstantial will* of God occurs when Satan shoots "flaming arrows" at us (Ephesians 6:16) to thwart our witness in order that someone will stumble. This persecution may be verbal, physical, or mental.

God's *ultimate will* is yet to be established, but it is sure to come. God's will occurs when the believer receives God's sustaining grace and refuses to give up.

Suffering That Comes from Theological Ignorance

Bad theology can prevent someone from understanding the will of God. A classic example of this is the biblical character of Job. The book of Job is perhaps the greatest drama ever written and is also an example of the pain that comes from a theology of ignorance. The prologue (Job 1–2) is key to understanding the dilemma that Job faced. Because he was not privy to the conversation between God and Satan, he had no clue as to why he was suffering. After all, he was a righteous man (Job 1:1). When test time came, he found it difficult to negotiate the mystery of his discomfort (Job 2:1-10). While momentary suffering is a challenge, the intensification of it can cause the best of us to complain bitterly. Satan, with God's permission, had attacked Job in three areas: his property, his family, and his body. At first, Job refused to call the integrity of God into question. Later on, however, we see that for Job, the onset of suffering was easier to handle than suffering that is prolonged. "After this, Job opened his mouth and cursed the day of his birth" (Job 3:1).

What brought on this about-face? The answer lies in the fact that Job's faith was influenced by his own theological ignorance and that of his friends. Both Job and his friends believed that good people should not have to suffer. Because he had money and morality, his situation was intensified. Job and his friends suffered from the same bad theology that many Christians suffer from today: If we are not receiving what we perceive to be life's best, then we must have done something wrong and therefore be out of God's will. It is almost impossible to understand God's will for our lives when we have a confused understanding of God.

Many Christians today are disturbed because many things that they have prayed for have not come to pass. They have bought into a false theology that is a cruel taskmaster. A theology that refuses all medical aid is sick. A theology that believes that all Christians will be rich is fantasy. Often, we cannot see God's will for our lives because we always look for God in that which is strong but never in that which is weak. We often miss God because we look for God in that which is exalted but never in that which is despised. God's love is not diminished by problems, pain, disappointment, disease, or death. God is Lord—period.

In the case of Job, God's *intentional will* was that he prosper, be blessed, and grow in his understanding of who God is. Job's preconceptions did not square with what he was going through. In other words, bad theology caused him great pain. The *circumstantial will* of God disrupted the rhythm of prosperity in Job's life. Job suffered when God and Satan made a deal without Job's consent. This caused Job great pain and anguish. Many doubts crept into his mind as he struggled to know God's will for his life. Hampered by a theology that could not cope with suffering, he was devastated.

In the epilogue, God finally established his *ultimate will* in Job's life. Job never received a philosophical response to his questions about suffering. Instead, he was blessed by the presence of God, which made further questions unnecessary. Job discovered that the God he had been looking for never existed. His future was brighter than his luxurious past because his doctrine of God had been clarified. Job's suffering was a school of learning. He learned that the path to paradise encounters both pleasure and pain, and God is never far away.

Suffering as Preparation for Promotion

Each of us would prefer to achieve our goals uncontested, but usually that will not be the case. In many instances, what we are going through is designed to get us to where God wants us to be. Many of us will never fulfill our destinies, because we want to arrive unscathed. Many churches have grown rapidly in the last twenty years because they have bought into this fantasy and their congregants have accepted it with open arms. We must remember that the butterfly was a struggling worm before it learned to fly. As the creature struggles to free itself, the tension brought by the cocoon causes wings to grow. When one sees the worm struggling, the first impulse is to free it from its situation. However, whoever would do so would rob the worm of its destiny of flying. In our own lives, we may be struggling in a cocoon and praying for deliverance. But God, seeing that releasing us from the struggle would hinder us from our destiny, might not answer our prayer for freedom.

Whenever we deal with suffering and the will of God, we must always place the wisdom of God over any other consideration. Fortunately, God does not answer all of our prayers according to our asking. God's will for our lives is higher ground, but we will not get there without a struggle.

The biblical character Daniel is an example of a person promoted through suffering. Daniel lived in seventh century B.C.E. He was carried into captivity by the Babylonians around 605 B.C.E. and was chosen (with his three friends Shadrach, Meshach, and Abednego), by order of the king, as one of a group of young Hebrew men to learn the Babylonian language and customs and to serve in the palace (Daniel 1:1-7). For Daniel, the Babylonian exile, though painful, was the first step in his ultimate promotion as a leader in a hostile land.

In the same way, were it not for the institution of slavery in America from 1619 until 1865, antislavery freedom fighters such as Denmark Vesey, Gabriel Prosser, Nat Turner, Sojourner Truth, Harriet Tubman, and Frederick Douglass would never have been called as leaders in a struggle. Like Daniel, they became leaders in a hostile land. Rather than being broken by their experience of slavery, these African American giants stand out like Daniel in their courage in facing an overwhelming situation. And, like Daniel, their situation was not by their own design.

The question for Daniel was not "Why am I suffering?" but rather "How must I respond to suffering?" Many times, when we suffer, our integrity is revealed. Does the pain diminish us or does it push us on to our rendezvous with destiny? For Daniel, the first test after being exiled was the king's menu.

But Daniel resolved not to defile himself with the royal food and wine, and he asked the chief official for permission not to defile himself this way. . . . Daniel then said . . . "Please test your servants for ten days: Give us nothing but vegetables to eat and water to drink. Then compare our appearance with that of the young men who eat the royal food." . . . At the end of the ten days they [Daniel and his three friends] looked healthier and better nourished than any of the young men who ate the royal food. So the guard took away their choice food and the wine they were to drink and gave them vegetables instead. (Daniel 1:8,11-13,15-16)

God's will is known through struggle. Daniel might never have grown had it not been for the suffering and struggles in his life. His courage to challenge what would have been harmful to his faith commitment prodded him on in his pilgrimage to know God's will. An indicator of authentic humanity is when we can stand even as we are being knocked down. And even in the midst of discomfort, each of us must recognize having been blessed with gifts, and that these gifts are strengthened through pain.

To these four young men [Daniel, Shadrach, Meshach, and Abednego] God gave knowledge and understanding of all kinds of literature and learning. And Daniel could understand visions and dreams of all kinds. At the end of the time set by the king . . . , the king talked with them, and he found none equal to Daniel [and his three friends]; so they entered the king's service. (Daniel 1:17-19)

Because of Daniel's gifts, he ended up in the employ of the king. In spite of the pain of being a slave in an oppressive situation, his gift made room for him. Yet even though Daniel continued to be promoted (Daniel 5:7,26-29), he was still conscious of the continuing struggle of a hostile environment. Daniel was no "Uncle Tom." He was making the best of a bad situation. Then, as now, it was impossible to harmonize God's ways with the prevailing culture. Likewise today, we must take a stand either for culture or for Christ, and the decision is never easy. In Daniel's case, the officials of Babylon set out to destroy him. Yet God was still with him.

Daniel did his job so well that the king planned to put him in charge of the entire kingdom. The other officials became extremely jealous, and being unable to find fault with his work, they decided to find fault with his faith. The officials convinced the king to issue a decree that required everyone to pray only to the king for thirty days. Anyone who prayed other than to the king would be thrown into the lions' den. In this emotionally charged situation, the question for Daniel was, "Do I choose the king or the King?" Daniel's choice of God over the king of Babylon caused him to end up in a lions' den (Daniel 6:3-16).

> At the first light of dawn, the king got up and hurried to the lions' den. When he came near the den, he called to Daniel in an anguished voice, "Daniel, servant of the living God, has your God, whom you serve continually, been able to rescue you from the lions?" Daniel answered, "O king, live forever! My God sent his angel, and he shut the mouths of the lions. They have not hurt me, because I was found innocent in his sight." . . . The king was overjoyed and gave orders to lift Daniel out of the den. And when Daniel was lifted from the den, no wound was found on him, because he had trusted in his God. (Daniel 6:19-23)

What we consider to be a curse can be a blessing in disguise. Our problems may turn out to be not in the stressful situations but in our successes. We may struggle to get a promotion, but once we achieve it, we are not immune to future challenges. The struggle gives us a chance to prove that God is real.

Therefore, we can conclude that it was not God's *intentional will* for the Jewish people to be enslaved by the Babylonians. Because of their transgressions, the good suffered with the bad. God's goal for Daniel was leadership. This is what God intended for him.

The *circumstantial will* of God is demonstrated by the enslavement of Daniel and his people. Because of slavery, God's will for Daniel was not postponed but accelerated. As a result of slavery, his character, courage, gifts, integrity, and witness were exemplified. Not even a hostile and oppressive situation can defeat the purposes of God. The *ultimate will* of

God did not change Daniel's slave situation. Rather, his situation gave him an opportunity to demonstrate the power of God. Even in our periods of suffering, we must thank God for our prosperity *and* for our pain.

Suffering as Retribution

Sometimes suffering comes and we can blame neither God nor Satan. It is because of what we have done. There is a law of reciprocity in the moral universe.

"Do not be deceived. . . . A man reaps what he sows. The one who sows to please his sinful nature, from that nature will reap destruction; the one who sows to please the Spirit, from the Spirit will reap eternal life" (Galatians 6:7-8).

This does not mean that we reap the same thing in kind (although sometimes that may happen). Essentially, it means that there is only one of two ways we can reap: either after the flesh or after the Spirit. Each of us has the power to decide what we will reap.

In America today, the violence that is so prevalent in almost every aspect of our culture is a derivative of our psyche of violence. As a nation, we were conceived and shaped in violence: we came into existence by violent revolution. How else can we explain our nation's decimation of Native Americans or the psychological crippling of African Americans? Given these roots, "They sow the wind and reap the whirlwind" (Hosea 8:7) is a good explanation for the state of today's violent society in America.

King David is a biblical example of someone who suffered as a consequence of his own sin, when he committed adultery with Bathsheba and had her husband, Uriah, killed in battle (2 Samuel 11). Because of his sin, David suffered greatly in several ways: (1) his conscience; (2) perpetual military and social chaos; (3) the death of his child born to Bathsheba; (4) the agony of his son Absalom, who slept with his concubines; and (5) the continued social stigma of his sin with Bathsheba.

Because David was out of God's will, he brought suffering to others, and therefore suffered himself. But because he was open to the prophetic word, he gained insight into the rationale for his suffering and therefore he did not complain about the injustice of his situation.

Suffering as Discipline

Suffering, from this perspective, is a blessing in disguise. A child who touches a hot stove learns, through the discipline of suffering, that this is something that should not be done. On June 27, 1999, I suffered congestive heart failure, which hospitalized me for sixteen days. During this time, I had a chance to confront the issue of my mortality. As a result of this, I am more health-conscious than I have ever been. At the time of this writing, I am enrolled in a medically supervised exercise and diet program. Did I enjoy being sick? No! But as a result of this experience, I can be a more effective kingdom vessel than I have ever been. No sane person enjoys pain in a masochistic sense. However, when we are in God's will, we are empowered to glory in tribulation (see Romans 5:3). Great good can come of, as well as in spite of, the discomfort of suffering.

> During the days of Jesus' life on earth, he offered up prayers and petitions with loud cries and tears to the one who could save him from death, and he was heard because of his reverent submission. Although he was a son, he learned obedience from what he suffered. (Hebrews 5:7-8)

This Scripture is saying that as a result of suffering, Jesus was helped, rather than hindered, by what he encountered. Therefore, he was able to interpret the Father's will for his life. What, then, did Jesus suffer?

- He suffered the indignity of being born in a barn, in the midst of animals (Luke 2:6-7).
- He suffered the stigma of being born and reared in the small, seemingly insignificant towns of Bethlehem and Nazareth (Luke 2:1-20,39).

- He suffered the stigma of a common vocation: carpenter (Mark 6:3).

- He suffered the rejection of his people, many of whom rejected him because he failed to be what they had projected him to be: a political/military messiah (John 1:11).

- He suffered at the hands of the political and religious coalitions of his day (Luke 19:47; 24:20).

- He suffered because of the defection of some of his disciples (John 6:66).

- He suffered through his death on the cross (Hebrews 13:12).

And, what did Jesus gain as a result of this suffering? The greatest gift of all:

> Therefore, God exalted him to the highest place and gave him the name that is above every name, that at the name of Jesus every knee should bow, in heaven and on earth and under the earth, and every tongue confess that Jesus Christ is Lord to the glory of God the Father. (Philippians 2:9-11)

Suffering That Proves Christian Character

Suffering is an opportunity for true Christian character to be demonstrated. When taken from this perspective, it is easier to discern God's will for our lives through suffering. While there is a retributive dimension to suffering, suffering is at its apex when it prods us along in the development of character. It is impossible to embrace the Judeo-Christian faith without coming to grips with suffering and its benefits.

The apostle Paul saw his "thorn in the flesh" as a painful, uncomfortable asset in the development of humility in his life. While we cannot know with certainty the nature of Paul's suffering, we do know that he believed that God was still accomplishing the divine will through his pain.

> To keep me from becoming conceited because of these surpassingly great revelations, there was given me a thorn in my flesh, a

messenger of Satan, to torment me. Three times I pleaded with
the Lord to take it away from me. But he said to me, "My grace is
sufficient for you, for my power is made perfect in weakness."
Therefore I will boast all the more gladly about my weaknesses, so
that Christ's power may rest on me. That is why, for Christ's
sake, I delight in weaknesses, in insults, in hardships, in persecu-
tions, in difficulties. For when I am weak, then I am strong. (2
Corinthians 12:7-10)

This is a declaration of faith that is radically different from
the popular Christianity of today. Early on, Paul was frustrated by his pain and saw no rhyme or reason for it. But
because of his pain, he was moved to another dimension
where it all made sense. In this Scripture, Paul teaches us
some basic principles that he learned as he sought God's will
through his pain. First, God permits some pain in order to
help us keep a level head, because we can easily become arrogant as a result of having received God's blessings. Second,
God does not always answer our prayers in the affirmative.
Sometimes, God says no. When that happens, we ought to be
grateful for the negative as well as the positive answers to
prayer. Third, God's sustaining grace is all-sufficient. It can
be more powerful than a miraculous deliverance, for God's
sufficient grace is a miracle within itself.

Suffering That Bears Witness

The person who is able to negotiate his or her suffering without giving up or giving out is a tremendous witness for the
kingdom of God. The Christian faith originally was a dangerous affair. There were many martyrs who gladly suffered
because they believed that through their actions many would
be turned toward God. The first of these was Stephen.

But Stephen, full of the Holy Spirit, looked up to heaven and saw
the glory of God, and Jesus standing at the right hand of God.
"Look," he said. "I see heaven open and the Son of Man standing
at the right hand of God." At this they covered their ears and,
yelling at the top of their voices, they all rushed at him, dragged

him out of the city and began to stone him. Meanwhile, the witnesses laid their clothes at the feet of a young man named Saul. While they were stoning him, Stephen prayed, "Lord Jesus, receive my spirit." Then he fell on his knees and cried out, "Lord, do not hold this sin against them." When he had said this, he fell asleep. (Acts 7:55-60)

The greatest gift that came as a result of the martyrdom of Stephen was its impact upon Saul, who was an accomplice to his murder. Was it God's will for Stephen to die? God's *intentional will* was for those who heard the testimony of Stephen to come to the knowledge of Jesus Christ. But, because they rejected his words, God's *circumstantial will* was his being stoned to death. But in spite of his death, God's *ultimate will* was established through the impression that it made upon the conscience of Saul of Tarsus.

Saul, who later would use his Latin name, Paul, became the greatest ambassador of the Christian faith. In the larger sense, Stephen died in order that Paul might live. Because Stephen transcended his situation of suffering, Paul also learned transcendence from Stephen and Jesus, for he too would suffer the fate of the martyr (2 Timothy 4:6-8). Paul's witness consequently laid the foundation for the theological expression of the Christian faith. Because of him, multiple millions have embraced the Christian cause, but it would not have happened without the profound witness of Stephen. This witness of a suffering man set Paul up to have his ultimate encounter with the Suffering One, the Risen Lord, on his way to Damascus (Acts 9:1-20). Therein lies the profound power of suffering in establishing God's will.

CHAPTER 5

Failure and Rejection

GOD DOES NOT ALWAYS DECLARE THE DIVINE WILL IN THE affirmative. Sometimes, life's negatives are profoundly positive and are rich with nuggets of gold, which we eventually find if we do not give up too soon. Trial and error is the stuff of which life is made. God makes the divine will known through success and failure. It is said that Thomas Alva Edison, "the Wizard of Menlo Park," made two thousand attempts before getting an electric light to burn consistently. He did not view these attempts as failures, which conjures up the notion of hopelessness. Rather, he saw them as revelations. In failure, he discovered what would not work. But he tried again and again, and the results we all know well.

Abraham Lincoln's remarkable record is peppered with ventures that failed: He lost his job in 1832; he was defeated for the legislature in 1832; he was elected to the legislature in 1834; he lost his sweetheart to death in 1835; he had a nervous breakdown in 1836; he failed in business in 1838; he was defeated for Speaker of the House in 1838; he was defeated for a congressional nomination in 1843; he was elected to Congress in 1846; he lost renomination in 1848; he was defeated for the Senate in 1854; he was defeated for a vice-presidential nomination in 1856; he was defeated for the Senate again in 1858; but he was elected president of the United States in 1860.

The lives of Edison and Lincoln are a commentary on the reality of life itself: it is a beautiful rhythm of ups and downs. Therefore, if we are going to understand God's will, we must adjust ourselves to the ebb and flow of life's tides. There are failures to be experienced in our pursuit of God's will.

Failure as a Signal of the Need for a Deeper Relationship with God

When the Israelites began the conquest of Canaan, they won a resounding victory at Jericho. There was great exuberance and joy. It is never difficult to declare God's love when we are doing well. However, when we fail personally or collectively, we recoil and begin to accuse God of malfeasance. We must not arrogantly assume that because we have triumphed at Jericho, we will always win, but neither must we conclude that God's will is final when we have failed.

> Now Joshua sent men from Jericho to Ai . . . and told them, "Go up and spy out the region." So the men went up and spied out Ai. When they returned to Joshua, they said, "Not all the people will have to go up against Ai. Send two or three thousand men to take it and do not weary all the people, for only a few men are there." So about three thousand men went up; but they were routed by the men of Ai. . . . Then Joshua tore his clothes and fell facedown to the ground. . . . And Joshua said, "Ah, Sovereign LORD, why did you ever bring this people across the Jordan to deliver us into the hands of the Amorites to destroy us?" . . . The Lord said to Joshua, "Stand up! What are you doing down on your face? Israel has sinned; they have violated my covenant, which I commanded them to keep." (Joshua 7:2-4,6-7,10-11)

God's *intentional will* was for Israel to defeat the city of Ai. But because of one man's sin in claiming booty from the conquered city of Jericho (Joshua 7:1), God's *circumstantial will* kicked in, which led to God permitting Israel to be defeated. But when that sinful man, Achan, was destroyed, God's *ultimate will* for Ai, complete destruction, was accomplished (Joshua 7:24-8:28).

Failure Can Be the Prelude to Victory

Toni Morrison's first novel was turned down several times before she found a publisher in 1970. Even then, it was not a commercial success. However, she kept writing and publishing, and in 1993 she became the first black woman to win the Nobel Prize for literature.

The great Scottish leader Robert Bruce, after having been discouraged in battle, withdrew in apparent defeat. But then, after observing the meticulous care and patience with which a spider wove its web, he was inspired to go back and win the battle.

Likewise, Jesus, at the beginning of his ministry, said to a distraught fisherman named Simon Peter, who had fished all night without catching anything, "Go back and try again."

> When [Jesus] had finished speaking, he said to Simon, "Put out into deep water, and let down the nets for a catch." Simon answered, "Master, we've worked hard all night and haven't caught anything. But because you say so, I will let down the nets." When they had done so, they caught such a large number of fish that their nets began to break. So they signaled their partners in the other boat to come and help them, and they came and filled both boats so full that they began to sink. When Simon Peter saw this, he fell at Jesus' knees and said, "Go away from me, Lord; I am a sinful man!" For he and his companions were astonished at the catch of fish they had taken, and so were James and John, the sons of Zebedee, Simon's partners. Then Jesus said to Simon, "Don't be afraid; from now on you will catch men." So they pulled their boats up on shore, left everything and followed him. (Luke 5:4-11).

Fishing, like living, is often frustrating. However, our failures can be windows of opportunity for God to establish the divine will. In the process, God has other lessons to teach us about how we can participate in the determination of God's ultimate decisions. Luke 5:1-11 teaches many lessons about failure and the discovery of God's will.

Lesson 1 Past experiences do not diminish today's possibilities. Even though we may have "toiled all night," we must remember that today offers new opportunities.

Lesson 2 We must not give in to our despair. While we are getting ready to give up, God is getting the divine will done.

Lesson 3 There are fish in the sea, even if there are not any in the boat. There is a thin line between a boat that's empty and a boat that's full.

Lesson 4 Perpetual failure can often be the result of our arrogance. Jesus was a carpenter who was telling a veteran fisherman where to find fish. This was a challenge to Peter's ego and to his humility. Sometimes God moves outside the expected order of things in order to accomplish the divine will.

Lesson 5 We can be blessed economically when we make an adjustment based upon the word of God. Peter was a career fisherman. That was his livelihood. But at the command of Jesus, he makes the necessary adjustment, and on the heels of failure, finds success.

Lesson 6 The willingness to receive instruction helps us to cope with failure while we work and wait to know God's will. Jesus *taught* Peter before he ordered him.

Lesson 7 God's will can be discovered when we move from the Word to the world. When we move from learning to living, we will gain greater insight into God's will.

Lesson 8 At least Peter and the others were in the vicinity of the problem and the possibility. Peter had failed, but he had not yet left the lake. He was getting ready to leave but had not left.

Lesson 9 Jesus meets us at the point of our frustration in order to sustain us as we wait to see his will taking place. Jesus set up a classroom right in the middle of the fishermen's point of failure.

Lesson 10 Although Peter had failed, he was not finished. What Peter thought could not be done, Jesus commanded him to do. There were fish to be caught in spite of, and because of, failure.

Lesson 11 Obedience is necessary in order to find God's will for our lives. When we obey God, all sorts of possibilities open up for us, and the stage is set for a showdown between failure and our future.

Failure That Comes after Victory

The story of the prophet Elijah's victory on Mount Carmel (1 Kings 18:16-46) and his subsequent despair (1 Kings 19:1-18) describes the tension and reality of living in this world. Elijah felt that he had forever driven a nail into the coffin of the false gods and prophets of Baal that had been perpetuated by Jezebel, but his victory was short-lived. He who had been fearless of 850 prophets of Baal was now running for his life because of the threat of Jezebel.

> Now Ahab told Jezebel everything Elijah had done and how he had killed all the prophets [of Baal] with the sword. So Jezebel sent a messenger to Elijah to say, "May the gods deal with me, be it ever so severely, if by this time tomorrow I do not make your life like one of them." Elijah was afraid and ran for his life. When he came to Beersheba in Judah, he left his servant there, while he himself went a day's journey into the desert. He came to a broom tree, sat down under it and prayed that he might die. (1 Kings 19:1-4)

In every life there are Mount Carmel periods of great joy, and post–Mount Carmel periods of moving from joy to sorrow, from exhilaration to exhaustion. What can we learn from this story, which discloses a deeper knowledge of the will of God? First, God wanted Elijah to "chill." Many times, we are so run down that we are running on fumes rather than on real energy. So, if we will not rest, God will permit situations and circumstances to evolve that will force us to rest. God wanted to keep Elijah from overestimating himself; God's will was for Elijah to understand that our victories are ours only when we recognize that they are God's. Elijah was victorious on Mount Carmel only because he participated in God's victory.

God also wanted Elijah to understand that there are heights beyond Mount Carmel. Mount Carmel is great, but to be with the Lord is the ultimate victory. Perhaps just as important, God wanted Elijah to accept the fact that we do not win every battle. Elijah never won Ahab and Jezebel over to the God of Israel. Finally, God's purpose was to get Elijah ready to prepare Elisha to be his successor.

Rejection is a necessary part of being human. Even the life of Jesus was one of defeats as well as victories. When God became incarnate in Jesus of Nazareth, this situation remained the same. After Jesus was victorious over the devil while fasting in the wilderness, he traveled to his hometown of Nazareth. There, he was not met with a hero's welcome. Instead, he was soundly rejected. In fact, the townspeople did not stop at kicking him out of town but even tried to throw him off a cliff (Luke 4:28-30)!

Rejection Often Discloses God's Will to Bless Others

Oftentimes, rejection by one group results in blessings for others. The rejection of Jesus in his hometown of Nazareth was a blessing for Capernaum.

The rejection of Jesus by his own people eventually opened the door for universal redemption. This theme is further emphasized by Pauline theology. Because of the rejection of the gospel by a majority of the Jews, salvation was opened to the Gentiles.

"I do not want you to be ignorant of this mystery, brothers, so that you may not be conceited: Israel has experienced a hardening in part until the full number of the Gentiles has come in" (Romans 11:25).

This Scripture simply underscores what was at the core of Old Testament theological teaching with regard to election. It was God's *intentional will* that the world be saved through the light that shone through the Jewish faith. When Israel confused privilege with responsibility, God's will was delayed but not defeated.

Not only did the apostle Paul discover God's will theologically, but also he found God's will in the rejection that he received in his own ministry. When he was rejected in Thessalonica, he went to Berea. "Now the Bereans were of more noble character than the Thessalonians, for they received the message with great eagerness and examined the Scriptures every day to see if what Paul said was true" (Acts 17:11). He had mixed results with the intellectual Athenians, and it was at Corinth that he felt the pain of rejection and made a decision that it was not God's immediate will to remain there. But, he was overruled.

> But when the Jews opposed Paul and became abusive, he shook out his clothes in protest and said to them, "Your blood be on your own heads! I am clear of my responsibility. From now on I will go to the Gentiles." . . . One night the Lord spoke to Paul in a vision: "Do not be afraid; keep on speaking, do not be silent. For I am with you, and no one is going to attack and harm you, because I have many people in this city." So Paul stayed for a year and a half, teaching them the word of God. (Acts 18:6,9-11)

As we seek to know God's will in the midst of rejection, we must be sensitive to God's timing.

Failure and Our Giftedness

"A gift opens the way for the giver and ushers him into the presence of the great" (Proverbs 18:16).

There are degrees of giftedness, from no gift at all in a particular area all the way to being profoundly gifted in a certain area. We must pray to know the difference as we seek to discern God's will. It is safe to say that baseball greats Sammy Sosa and Ken Griffey Jr. will not be invited to lecture at Morehouse College in the area of philosophy. Such an assignment would be an abysmal failure. On the other hand, while Martin Luther King Jr. and Howard Thurman excelled in philosophy, neither would have made it on the professional baseball field. Our particular gifts help us to understand God's will for our lives. We are blessed when we make this discovery, for then the Lord who gives us these gifts will be glorified.

CHAPTER 6

Patience

IT IS TROUBLING, SOMETIMES, WHEN PROVIDENCE DEMANDS that we must wait. We live in the age of instant messaging, microcomputers, and nanoseconds. We deem it imperative that we get what we want, when we want it, and where we want it—right now! Even our self-centered brand of Christianity declares that we have a "covenant right" to have what we want, whenever we want it. In other words, God must move when we call. Sometimes God does move instantaneously, but by and large, we will usually discover the divine will through patience.

> Do you not know? Have you not heard? The LORD is the everlasting God, the Creator of the ends of the earth. He will not grow tired or weary, and his understanding no one can fathom. He gives strength to the weary and increases the power of the weak. Even youths grow tired and weary, and young men stumble and fall; but those who hope in the LORD will renew their strength. They will soar on wings like eagles; they will run and not grow weary, they will walk and not be faint. (Isaiah 40:28-31)

The two main words for "patience" in the Greek New Testament are *hypomone* and *makrothymia*. *Hypomone* has to do with putting up with difficult situations, and literally means "to abide under the load." *Makrothymia* literally means "the ability to handle a lot of heat" and is, in reality, long-suffering. Many times we confuse stoicism, which is the freezing of one's emotions, with patience. Patience does not mean that we should never complain (although we do complain too much).

> Brothers, as an example of patience in the face of suffering, take the prophets who spoke in the name of the Lord. As you know, we consider blessed those who have persevered. You have heard of Job's perseverance and have seen what the Lord finally brought about. (James 5:10-11)

In this letter, Job's perseverance is held up as a model for Christian practice. People often speak of the "patience of Job" as if Job never complained throughout his ordeal. But this belief is invalidated by the book of Job itself. Job does nothing but complain, but yet he waited (Job 14:14).

I grew up on a fifty-two acre farm outside of Ocala, Florida. One day, my father told me to pick up a twenty-pound sack of grain for the cattle. I was only about eight years old at the time. I had to carry the bag of grain about twenty yards in order to reach the barn. I wondered to myself, since my dad was bigger and stronger, why didn't he just carry it himself? He said to me, "Son, this will help to make you into a man." So, I grabbed the sack and immediately started to complain, but I finally made it to the barn and dropped the sack at my father's feet. That was a lesson in patience. Patience means that you stay with the task no matter how difficult. It is about *hypomone,* "abiding under the load."

Makrothymia, or long-suffering, is used in the sense of negotiating with difficult people. Every pastor-teacher needs long-suffering. My first recollection of a preacher was Charles Henry Rhodes (1867–1969), who pastored one congregation for over sixty years. He was a very meek man. For years, he had to endure many hostile and belligerent members, but he never fought back. Mean-spirited officers of the church would arbitrarily deduct money from his meager salary to help defray church expenses. He would only say, "They must have needed it." This godly man is a tremendous example of patience. Because he waited in every situation, God brought him through the storms.

Likewise, as we determine to know God's will, we must buy into the power that comes through patience. People of faith will encounter many things that will cause frustration, but maturing believers are conscious of the fact that God is responsible for their past deliverances.

We will now explore some of the benefits to be derived from waiting on God as we seek to know the divine will.

Time Makes God's Will Clear

The anxiety of waiting on time is, actually, a quiet blessing as we pray to know God's will. Sometimes we say in our spirits, and sometimes rebelliously, "God, why is it taking you so long?" We don't like to wait, and it may take years for God's will to come to pass.

> Then the LORD replied: "Write down the revelation and make it plain on tablets so that a herald may run with it. For the revelation awaits an appointed time; it speaks of the end and will not prove false. Though it linger, wait for it; it will certainly come and will not delay." (Habakkuk 2:2-3)

For all the power of this awesome prophecy, it would take seventy years for it to come to pass. However, it did come to pass in the defeat of the Babylonian Empire. Sometimes the tenure of waiting can become so depressing that we tend to give up. But if we can wait, knowing that "he who does all things well" will work it out, we will be better for having waited.

The person of Abraham looms large in salvation history as someone who was perpetually in search of God's will. God promised to bless the world through Abraham's posterity even though Abraham did not have a son. To make matters more incredible, Abraham was already seventy-five years old.

> The LORD said to Abram, "Leave your country, your people and
> your father's household and go to the land I will show you. I will
> make you into a great nation and I will bless you; I will make your
> name great, and you will be a blessing. I will bless those who bless
> you, and whoever curses you I will curse; and all peoples on earth
> will be blessed through you." . . . Abram was seventy-five years
> old when he set out from Haran. (Genesis 12:1-4)

We live in a culture where the aged are conditioned both by
culture and by physical reality to give up at a certain time.
But God works in the lives of the elderly, as well as the
young. As if being seventy-five were not enough, Abraham
would have to wait twenty-five years to see the fulfillment of
God's will for his life. Many things would transpire in his life
before the promise would come to pass.

In the case of Abraham, an intervening blessing came in
the form of a son, Ishmael. Sarah, not believing that she
would ever bear a child, encouraged Abraham to have one by
her servant, Hagar. Hagar conceived, and she bore Abraham
a son, Ishmael.

Many times we can miss a promised blessing because of
the overwhelming significance of an intervening blessing.
Even though Ishmael arrived fourteen years earlier than
Isaac, it would have been easy for the elderly Abraham to
become complacent and satisfied and to declare that God's
will had already been done. Ishmael was important, but he
was not the fulfillment of God's will. Abraham believed God;
he knew that Sarah would bear a child.

> Now the LORD was gracious to Sarah as he had said, and the
> LORD did for Sarah what he had promised. Sarah became preg-
> nant and bore a son to Abraham in his old age, at the very time
> God had promised him. Abraham gave the name Isaac to the
> son Sarah bore him. When his son Isaac was eight days old,
> Abraham circumcised him, as God commanded him. Abraham
> was a hundred years old when his son Isaac was born to him.
> (Genesis 21:1-5)

No matter how long we wait, what God has promised will
come to pass. If we can be patient, the will of God can be
accomplished in our lives.

Through Patience, Character Is Developed

What God's *circumstantial will* allows us to go through works together so that God's *ultimate will* may be fulfilled. While waiting, we will encounter hurt and pain. But we will discover that in the process of moving toward our God-directed goals, time offers us healing for our pain. As our character is being developed through patience, we avoid many errors. Many times, our lives are an ongoing cacophony of perpetual confusion because we do not pause long enough to discern God's will.

There are many concerns that ought to be worked out through patience and prayer, such as: What college should I attend? Whom should I date? What is my life's vocation? What job should I take? Where should I live? What religious institution should I affiliate with? What God should I commit my life to? These are questions that do not jibe well with hasty, irrational responses. These and other concerns will take time. The reason our lives are often chaotic is that we refuse to wait until God's will is clarified.

Ted Williams is, by any gauge, one of the top five hitters in baseball history. In terms of average and power, only Josh Gibson and Babe Ruth would have been better. The thing that made Williams such a great hitter was the fact that he always waited to get a pitch in the strike zone that he could hit. That is the difference between mediocrity and the Hall of Fame—the patience to wait. Or consider Rubin "Hurricane" Carter, an excellent boxer who was unjustly accused of murder and spent over twenty years in prison before being released. How we respond to our pain is far more profound than the agony of the pain itself. Will I master my pain? Or will my pain master me? Will I be imprisoned in my mind as well as in my body? Or will I allow my spirit to escape even the confines of prison bars? Rubin Carter eventually won his freedom. In spite of the tragedy of his imprisonment, Carter learned the power of *agape* love.

Through Patience, We Learn about God, Ourselves, and Others

Many of life's contradictions that force us to wait are our most profound instructors. While we are waiting, we are in school. While we are enrolled in the school of patience, the most important subject is God. We look at our situation and sometimes wonder, "Where is God in all of this? When is God going to make a move?"

Though Job waited in confusion, he learned in one class sitting who God is, who he himself is, and the character of his friends. Thinking emotionally, we declare that we know God, but when we have to wait through an ordeal, we may have to change our theology.

> Then Job replied to the LORD: "I know that you can do all things; no plan of yours can be thwarted. You asked, 'Who is this that obscures my counsel without knowledge?' Surely I spoke of things I did not understand, things too wonderful for me to know. You said, 'Listen now, and I will speak; I will question you, and you shall answer me.' My ears had heard of you but now my eyes have seen you. Therefore I despise myself and repent in dust and ashes." (Job 42:1-6)

Job endured his own interrogative state while Satan wreaked havoc, and God watched. Beyond this, he had to listen to the scathing analyses of his friends. But he stayed in school until the Master Teacher called for recess. As a result, Job learned many lessons that gave him insight into the will of God. While enrolled in the school of patience, he refused to give up the load. He did not "drop the sack." Therefore, in the process of waiting, he discovered God's will for his life. These are some of the lessons that Job learned while waiting on God:

- Authentic faith does not require us to deny reality.
- God is infinitely greater than one's alleged righteousness.
- Pain is more about discipline and discovery than it is about destruction.

- One's standing with God cannot be erased by the analyses of others.

- Nothing happens outside of God's love and care.

- Forgiveness is the medium through which God's intentional will, though interrupted by circumstances, finally comes to pass.

After Job prayed for his friends, the LORD made him prosperous again and gave him twice as much as he had before. All his brothers and sisters and everyone who had known him before came and ate with him in his house. . . . The Lord blessed the latter part of Job's life more than the first. He had fourteen thousand sheep, six thousand camels, a thousand yoke of oxen and a thousand donkeys. And he also had seven sons and three daughters. . . . After this, Job lived a hundred and forty years; he saw his children and their children to the fourth generation. And so he died, old and full of years. (Job 42:10-13,16-17)

Through Patience, Vocational Destinies Are Clarified

Running ahead of God is dangerous. Shakespeare's *Macbeth* offers a classic example of someone who was impatient and who paid with his life. Macbeth had to have his way—now.

The play is set in Scotland. Returning from battle with his companion Banquo, Macbeth meets some witches. They predict that Macbeth will first become Thane of Cawdor and then King of Scotland. Macbeth privately has had ambitions of being king. After the first part of the witches' prophecy comes true, he begins to think the second part may also come true. Encouraged by Lady Macbeth, his wife, Macbeth murders King Duncan, a guest in his castle. Macbeth then seizes the throne of Scotland. But Macbeth has no peace. Duncan's sons have escaped to England where they seek support against Macbeth. In addition, the witches had also predicted that Banquo's descendants would be kings of Scotland. Macbeth therefore orders the murder of Banquo and his son, Fleance. Macbeth's men kill Banquo. Macbeth is now hardened to killing. He orders the murder of the wife and children of his enemy Macduff, who had fled to England after

Duncan's murder. Macduff then gathers an army to overthrow Macbeth. By this time, Lady Macbeth, burdened with guilt over the murders, has become a sleepwalker. She finally dies. At the end of the play, Macduff kills Macbeth in battle. Duncan's son Malcolm is then proclaimed King of Scotland. (*World Book Encyclopedia,* vol. 17, p. 361)

Because Macbeth lacked patience, he allowed his ambition to get the best of him, and his life became a tragedy. The moral of this drama is that our impatience often can have a deleterious effect upon the lives of others. This drama is also a window into the lives of millions of people who end up in vocations and positions for which they are ill suited or for which the timing is wrong. Time is a precious gift that needs to be employed as we wait to discover God's will with regard to our life's vocation.

The story of King Saul and David is a model account of waiting for God's time. Saul, son of Kish, was Israel's first king. His life was as tragic as any that Shakespeare later devised. He occupied a position that he did not seek and that God did not want him to have. In other words, with regard to his vocation, Saul was never in God's *intentional will.* He was king by virtue of God's *circumstantial will.* Therefore, he never achieved his final destiny, because he was in the wrong vocation. After Saul ultimately was rejected by God (1 Samuel 15), the stage was set for the evolution of David as king of Israel.

In the interval between Saul's rejection and his demise at Gilboa (1 Samuel 31), we see the politics of God. In reality, by the providential politics of God, David actually was king before being crowned (1 Samuel 16:1-13). Many times, while we are plotting and looking out for ourselves, God has already moved on our behalf. David, like Saul, did not seek the office. He was satisfied being a shepherd and musician. David was not waiting to be crowned. He was waiting on God's timing. While David waited, he had much to deal with.

First, David had to deal with the politics of God, which placed him in a precarious and yet purposeful situation.

Things had happened so suddenly that he needed to "chill." Even though he had been anointed, he probably did not understand the full implication of what had happened to him. As would later be the case with Saul of Tarsus after his dramatic conversion, David needed a period of waiting and reflection. Any individual, no matter how gifted, needs a period of reflection before assuming an official position.

Second, David had to deal with the mental illness of Saul. He became the minister of music for Saul's manic depression. His music was a palliative for the king's madness (1 Samuel 16:14-23). David's anointing for the future did not hinder his creativity. It takes patience to wait our turn while others may consider us to be a flunky. In the providence of God, where we are currently is the best possible place that we can be at that time. The problem comes when we leap out of God's will and try to make our own destinies, paving the way for defeat.

Third, David had to deal with the jealousy of Saul (1 Samuel 18:1-29). Jealousy in any form puts one at the mercy of the Evil One. It is amazing how sometimes our good intentions can be spoken of as evil. David was not waiting to be king; he was not biting his nails or biding his time waiting to make the right move. He was satisfied serving the one who was king. But because the people sang higher praises of David than of King Saul, David became an enemy of the king. "And from that time on Saul kept a jealous eye on David" (1 Samuel 18:9).

Fourth, David had to deal with deceit, treachery, and attempted murder on the part of Saul (1 Samuel 19). As we wait on God in order to know the divine will, we often find ourselves in precarious positions from which it is very difficult to free ourselves. But even these dangerous encounters help to prepare us as we gain insight into the will of God. Self-preservation may be the first law of nature, but it is not the first law of the kingdom of God. "Seek first [God's] kingdom and his righteousness, and all these things will be given to you as well" (Matthew 6:33). This verse seems to go against the grain of any culture or civilization. Perhaps that is because it seems to be so nonaggressive—and it is, unless we see it as "aggressive patience." Aggressive patience can be defined as doing everything within our power to wait until God reveals the divine will for our lives. While David waited, he conducted himself with dignity and refused to let Saul dictate his response. David had a chance to kill Saul; he refused to do so (1 Samuel 24:1-7).

Patience makes us face the heat, and we are transformed by the experience. Patience is a mirror in which we are able to see our real selves. Certainly, while David waited, questions raced in and out of his mind. If God has rejected Saul, why didn't God just move him? If God has anointed David to be king, why didn't God eliminate Saul in order to establish the reign of David? Sometimes, as the will of God becomes clearer to us, we understand that oftentimes the rejected becomes an instructor for the accepted in order that the latter may know how not to behave. Negative experiences can have positive influences. Therefore, it was not God's will for David to kill Saul. Instead, God wanted David to learn from Saul. What did David learn through patience?

David learned that kings must never be petty. David never threw the fact of his anointing in Saul's face. He was comfortable waiting on Saul as God worked out the logistics of his coronation. David also learned that eluding an enemy is better than destroying one. David's defense was to outrun Saul. Although he had ample opportunity to kill Saul, David discovered God's will in refusing to take Saul's life. Although David was disappointed in the behavior of Saul, he never believed that his own success required that Saul be exterminated. Some things are best left to be handled by God. In God's time, David became king without murder, intrigue, or political maneuverings.

> In the course of time, David inquired of the LORD. "Shall I go up to one of the towns of Judah?" he asked. The LORD said, "Go up." David asked, "Where shall I go?" "To Hebron," the LORD

answered. So David went up there. . . . And there they anointed David king over the house of Judah. (2 Samuel 2:1-2,4)

Patience Helps Us to Understand the Principle of Seasons

If we can understand that life, like the natural order, is about the ebb and flow of seasons, we can go a long way toward understanding the will of God. In the botanical realm, plants and flowers grow and bloom only during their respective seasons. As we approach the season of young adulthood, our vertical growth comes to an end. The earth's seasons call for an orderliness that points us toward an orderly God. If spring always follows winter, and summer always follows spring, and if autumn always follows summer and precedes winter, then certain things can be deduced about the seasons of our lives.

> There is a time for everything, and a season for every activity under heaven: a time to be born and a time to die, a time to plant and a time to uproot, a time to kill and a time to heal, a time to tear down and a time to build, a time to weep and a time to laugh, a time to mourn and a time to dance, a time to scatter stones and a time to gather them, a time to embrace and a time to refrain, a time to search and a time to give up, a time to keep and a time to throw away, a time to tear and a time to mend, a time to be silent and a time to speak, a time to love and a time to hate, a time for war and a time for peace. . . . [God] has made everything beautiful in its time. (Ecclesiastes 3:1-8,11a)

The writer of these verses is not arguing for fatalism or predeterminism but instead is simply saying that life is like crossing a river. There are two shores, and life is lived in between. When we arrive at the other shore depends upon timing. What time did we leave? What obstacles did we encounter? As we try to determine the will of God, it is necessary to understand that life, sickness, and death are intricate parts of the seasons of life.

A season of defeat can be a prelude to a victorious life. Nelson Mandela, the South African antiapartheid freedom fighter, was imprisoned for twenty-five years because of his political activities. There were, surely, times when he thought that he would die in his cell. Yet by the time he was released from his confinement, he was an international hero and was later elected the first black president of the nation of South Africa.

Sometimes, one's season is brief and yet productive. Why does a Paul Laurence Dunbar, a Lorraine Hansberry, a Malcolm X, or a Martin Luther King Jr. die before the age of forty? It has to be because their season was over.

Understanding one's season is about knowing when to move and when to stay put. Moving either too soon or too late can be catastrophic. The Allied invasion of Normandy on northern France, which began on June 6, 1944, was a major turning point in World War II. This assault broke the Germans' grip on France and eventually drove them out. Once the invasion had been planned, the problem that confronted General Dwight D. Eisenhower was when to launch the attack. Because of bad weather, the Allies suffered postponements and had to wait until the right time. However, because the Allies had calculated correctly, the strategic maneuver was successful, and ultimately Hitler was defeated.

Patience Helps Us to Understand That We Are in Spiritual Warfare

We are in a battle, and the struggle between spiritual forces compels us to be patient.

"For our struggle is not against flesh and blood, but against the rulers, against the authorities, against the powers of this dark world and against the spiritual forces of evil in the heavenly realms" (Ephesians 6:12).

This struggle is not merely metaphorical; it is a reality. Many times, we wonder why it is taking so long for our ship to come in. The answer could reside in the fact that one's destiny is tied up or detained by spiritual warfare. Because of this, God's *intentional will* is slow in coming to pass. The intentional will is hindered for a time because of the principalities and powers, but God's *ultimate will* wins out. Unless we understand this struggle, we will miss an important ingredient in the understanding of God's will. The book of Daniel gives insight into this struggle for the realization of the divine will.

> A hand touched me and set me trembling on my hands and knees. He said, "Daniel, you are highly esteemed, consider carefully the words I am about to speak to you, and stand up, for I have now been sent to you." And when he said this to me, I stood up trembling. Then he continued, "Do not be afraid, Daniel. Since the first day that you set your mind to gain understanding and to humble yourself before God, your words were heard, and I have come in response to them. But the prince of the Persian kingdom resisted me twenty-one days. Then Michael, one of the chief princes, came to help me, because I was detained there with the king of Persia." (Daniel 10:10-13)

This passage talks about Daniel being placed in a position where he has to wait twenty-one days until he can get a breakthrough. Because he had to wait, he gained insight into the reality of principalities and powers. Like Daniel, who prayerfully waited, we too must understand the power of prayerfully waiting for the fulfillment of God's will. But while we are waiting, the war wages on until God's will is finally done.

Patience Gives Us a Chance to See God's Will Become Visible

In biblical faith, the phrase "and it came to pass" is pregnant with relief for the human situation. When life moves from the subjective to the objective, belief becomes knowledge. The ancient Hebrews are a powerful illustration of a people waiting, for 430 years, until their liberation became a visible, historical reality (Exodus 12:40-41). During this period of suffering, the people cried out to God. Even though the people called upon God for liberation, theirs was not to be immediate. However, this period of patience was a prelude to the actual exodus (Exodus 12–14). Therefore, the exodus became the watershed event in the sacred history of the Hebrews. The exodus, after a wait of 430 years, became the visible evidence of the pain of a people and of the power of God. Even though both God and the people were affected by their oppression, God, for whatever reason, acted in his own time. Therefore, the Hebrews could know the will of God only by waiting for their deliverance to become a visible reality. The exodus was the tangible expression of God's *intentional will* that they would return to the land of Canaan. Because of the slavery, under God *circumstantial will,* that required four centuries and three decades of patience, the *ultimate will* of God occurred forty years after the exodus whey they finally entered the land of Canaan under the leadership of Joshua (Joshua 2–3).

Patience Is Not Pious Inactivity

Patience, though sometimes painful, should never be boring. Doing nothing is not what patience is all about. Patience is about waiting as we work and pray. The Civil Rights movement in America is an example of this. There were many African Americans and white Americans who believed that the issue of race would be solved almost by osmosis if we patiently practiced gradualism. But things do not just happen because we do nothing. They happen when we creatively use our patience to effectuate the will of God. There were others who felt that violence was the way to go because America itself was established with a violent revolution. But along came Martin Luther King Jr., and others, who applied the principles of aggressive nonviolence, and radical changes were made in America. Dr. King was not just a "Jesus will fix it while we do nothing" kind of person. He believed that we should work together with God. The Civil Rights movement was about aggressive patience as many worked to see the universality of brotherhood and sisterhood. While Dr. King waited to see the fulfillment of God's will, which was justice for African Americans as well as for all people, many things happened to the civil rights workers: jailings, bombings, beatings, stabbings, and murders. Although Dr. King did not live to see God's *ultimate will* come to pass, he died believing that it would eventually come to pass.

The activity of patience has nothing to do with working to achieve one's goal through human instrumentality. It is about working to strengthen our faith as we patiently wait for God to clear away the impediments that prevent us from seeing God's will accomplished in our lives. Being patient does not mean being comatose.

Even in jail, Paul and Silas exercised an aggressive patience. They were imprisoned for casting out a demon from a girl who was a fortune-teller.

> She earned a great deal of money for her owners. . . . When the owners of the slave girl realized that their hope of making money was gone, they seized Paul and Silas and dragged them into the marketplace to face the authorities. . . . About midnight, Paul and Silas were praying and singing hymns to God, and the other prisoners were listening to them. . . . At once all the prison doors flew open, and everybody's chains came loose. (Acts 16:16b,19,25-26).

What Paul and Silas accomplished was far more potent than armed warfare in accomplishing God's will: the conversion of the Philippian jailer (Acts 16:27-34) and the establishment of the first church on European soil (Acts 16:11-15).

Patience Gives Us a Chance to Prepare for God's No

As we wait to know God's will, we must not let presumption take hold of our lives. Thank God for sometimes saying no! We are enchanted by and attracted to many things that we want. But sometimes those things are not God's will for our lives. The apostle Paul provides a corrective for us.

Paul and his companions traveled throughout the region of Phry-
gia and Galatia, having been kept by the Holy Spirit from preaching the word in the province of Asia. When they came to the
border of Mysia, they tried to enter Bithynia, but the Spirit of
Jesus would not allow them to. So they passed by Mysia and went
down to Troas. During the night Paul has a vision of a man of
Macedonia standing and begging him, "Come over to Macedonia
and help us." After Paul had seen the vision, we got ready at once
to leave for Macedonia, concluding that God had called us to
preach the gospel to them. (Acts 16:6-10)

After being rebuffed, not by human opposition, but by the
Holy Spirit, the apostle Paul found God's will not where he
wanted to be, but where God wanted him to be.

CHAPTER 7

Faith

NO SINGLE TOPIC ON THE BIBLICAL-THEOLOGICAL LANDSCAPE today is more confusing than that of the role of faith in our lives. The confusion arises because our notions of faith run the gamut from the "name it and claim it" belief system, which expects prayers to be answered by some sort of spiritual magic, all the way to purely intellectual assertions that faith is nothing more than acknowledging the existence of certain facts or occurrences. The Bible gives us a clear and concise definition of faith:

> Now faith is being sure of what we hope for and certain of what we do not see. This is what the ancients were commended for. By faith we understand that the universe was formed at God's command, so that what is seen was not made out of what was visible. (Hebrews 11:1-3)

Once we accept this definition, faith can be understood as surrendering to God's power, love, and reality. Then we are in a better position to interpret the will of God, because we understand that faith is a means of surrendering to, rather than subverting or ignoring, God's will.

Old Testament Examples of Faith

Abraham

In biblical history, Abraham (first called Abram) is a proto-type of faith. He moved out in faith in order to discover God's will for him and his family.

> The LORD had said to Abram, "Leave your country, your people and your father's household and go to the land I will show you." . . . So Abram left, as the LORD had told him. . . . He took his wife Sarai, his nephew Lot, all the possessions they had accumu-lated and the people they had acquired in Haran, and they set out for the land of Canaan, and they arrived there. (Genesis 12:1,4-5)

This call to Abraham was a call of destiny unseen. Yet it was also a move that first had been attempted by Abraham's father, Terah, many years before.

Long before Abraham heard the call from God, Terah set out from the country of Ur with Abraham, Sarah (first called Sarai), and the rest of his family, intending to go to Canaan. But when they reached Haran, they stopped and settled there. Terah died in the land of Haran (Genesis 11:31-32). What made Abraham's journey to Canaan different from that of his father? Perhaps the difference between Abraham and his father was that Abraham had a divine revelation and Terah did not. Terah was attempting to do what he wanted to do— go to Canaan. But Abraham accomplished his goal because of a divine mandate coupled with the faith that brought him to the completion of God's will for his life.

It is always dangerous for us to move out without God's directive. Sometimes, we can enjoy Haran so much that we cannot fulfill our destinies. Sometimes, we have enough faith to get us to Haran but not enough to get us to Canaan. In the case of Terah, perhaps it was God's *intentional will* for Terah to enter Canaan. However, it could be that the com-placency he felt in Haran prevented him from fulfilling God's *ultimate will* for his life. It is clear that it was God's *intentional will* that Abraham would do what his father, Terah, would not, could not, or was not supposed to do. Abraham moved out by faith, and God's *final will* began to be fulfilled when he arrived in Canaan. Abraham exercised faith in order to fulfill God's will for his life and to carry out God's universal purpose.

As we grow in faith, we will often be stretched to the limit of our ability to believe what God is going to do in our lives. However, if we do not move out by faith from where we are, we will never discover where we need to be and where God ultimately wants us to be. This was true in Abraham's life. After fulfilling the initial call of God's will upon his life, Abraham was ready for another faith challenge. This next level of faith involved both him and his wife and required that they believe that the Lord could work a miracle in their lives. When Abraham was ninety-nine years old and Sarah was eighty-nine years old, the Lord spoke to Abraham and told him that his wife would bear him a son by that time next year. "I will bless her so that she will be the mother of nations; kings of peoples will come from her" (Genesis 17:16b). Abraham was called upon to believe what appeared to be an impossibility. Yet by faith, Abraham did believe, and it happened just as the Lord promised. "The LORD did for Sarah what he had promised. Sarah became pregnant and bore a son to Abraham in his old age, at the very time God had promised him. Abraham gave the name Isaac to the son Sarah bore him" (Genesis 21:1-3).

Many of us have made an initial step of obedience, may even have experienced the miraculous, but still are not committed to God. Commitment is the greatest evidence of faith because it involves action. This level of commitment involves action on our part as a response to our faith that God's *ultimate will* will be done. "Faith without deeds is dead" (James 2:26). Abraham was called to sacrifice his son Isaac. Abraham was willing to do this even though he believed God, who said that many nations would come from him through Isaac.

When [Abraham and Isaac] reached the place God told him about, Abraham built an altar there and arranged the wood on it. He bound his son Isaac and laid him on the altar, on top of the wood. Then he reached out his hand and took the knife to slay his son. But the angel of the Lord called out to him from heaven, "Abraham! Abraham! . . . Do not lay a hand on the boy." (Genesis 22:9-12)

Then God provided a ram for the sacrifice in place of Isaac.

James 2:22 tells us that Abraham's "faith and his actions were working together, and his faith was made complete by what he did." When we act on God's word, by faith, we may be delayed, but we will not be disappointed—God's *ultimate will* prevails.

Joseph

We have already dealt with Joseph and his triumph of faith from the pit to the prison and from the prison to the palace (Genesis 37–46). It has already been established that God's *intentional will* was that Joseph be a blessing to his family, but the *circumstantial will* of God was demonstrated in the form of envy and jealousy on the part of his brothers. But finally, God's *ultimate will* was done. Beyond this, Joseph made another gesture of faith that was just as incredible. As he approached death, through the eyes of faith he was able to see liberation for his people before they were even enslaved!

Then Joseph said to his brothers, "I am about to die. But God will surely come to your aid and take you up out of this land to the land he promised on oath to Abraham, Isaac and Jacob." And Joseph made the sons of Israel swear an oath and said, "God will surely come to your aid, and then you must carry my bones up from this place." So Joseph died at the age of a hundred and ten. And after they embalmed him, he was placed in a coffin in Egypt. (Genesis 50:24-26)

By faith, the final will of God was established with the exodus event (Exodus 13–14), the relocation of Joseph's bones (Exodus 13:19), and their final burial at Shechem (Joshua 24:32).

Moses

Moses also was a great man of faith. By faith, Moses gave up his position of prestige and privilege in order to discover God's will outside pharaoh's palace as he identified with his oppressed brothers and sisters. It is ironic that the enslavement of the Hebrews was a direct result of God's *circumstantial will* in permitting the sons of Jacob to sell their brother Joseph into slavery (Genesis 37). Joseph, after surviving several stumbling blocks, ended up being a high official in the land of Egypt. After Joseph was exalted, a famine occurred. The famine caused Jacob and the brothers of Joseph to move to Egypt in order to avoid starvation (Genesis 46). The problem was not in going to Egypt, but in wearing out their welcome—they stayed too long. Then came a pharaoh who did not know Joseph (Exodus 1:8). As a result, the descendants of Jacob spent over four hundred years in slavery. This was not God's *intentional will.* God established plans and purposes with Abraham in Genesis 17:7-8. Due to the sin on the part of Joseph's brothers, manifested under the *circumstantial will* of God, God's *intentional will* was delayed, but it was not defeated. The exodus was the beginning of the fulfillment of God's *intentional will* that the Hebrews live in the land of Canaan. However, the exodus was only the prelude, for God's *ultimate will* would not occur under the leadership of Moses, but under his successor, Joshua (Joshua 3–4).

Jeremiah

Many times, the demands of faith seem to be ridiculous, but if we wait, God's *intentional will* is established in the end. A marvelous example of a seemingly absurd act of faith is found in the book of Jeremiah. Because Jeremiah prophesied Judah's defeat to the Babylonians, King Zedekiah ordered him placed under guard and confined to the royal palace. While Jeremiah was under arrest, the Lord again spoke to him, telling him to buy a field—a piece of land—and have the deed signed and witnessed by all of the Jews in the king's courtyard. "For this is what the LORD Almighty, the God of Israel, says: Houses, fields, and vineyards will again be bought in this land" (Jeremiah 32:15).

Why would Jeremiah buy land when he had just prophesied that the country was about to be taken over by a foreign power? Even though this message to the people of Judah was from the Lord, Jeremiah must have appeared to be a complete idiot. But the Lord was making a point with this absurd request: eventually, the people would return to their homeland and possess it with all of the rights to buy and sell and own that they originally had.

What can we say about Jeremiah's real estate deal? What can we say of faith when the situation seems to be ludicrous? Here are some principles we can learn from Jeremiah and his faith in God:

- Being a product of Western civilization, we close ourselves to the "ridiculous" requests of God. We prefer to accept what can be explained within the confines of logic. Yet when we are open, miraculous things can happen. Only through eyes of faith could Mary McLeod Bethune (1875–1955) have arrived in Daytona Beach, Florida, in 1904 with $1.50 in her purse and achieved her dream of starting a much-needed school for African American students.

- Faith is a problem if we are living only for ourselves. Jeremiah's act of faith was not a personal gesture but a statement about what God was doing in the present and what God was going to do in the future for the people of Judah.

- Faith embraces reality and then transforms it into the miraculous.

- Faith refuses to accept oppression as the *final will* of God. Faith says that the oppressor does not control us no matter how we perceive it. Even though the Babylonians were on the verge of conquering Judah, the prophet Jeremiah saw God, not Nebuchadnezzar, being in control.

- Faith says that our present condition must not keep us from having hope in tomorrow.
- Faith says that what once was can be again. Faith does not rest upon human perception but upon the promises of God.

The Three Hebrew Youth

Shadrach, Meshach, and Abednego, through their faith, discovered the will of God. They were about to be thrown into the fiery furnace as punishment for refusing to worship King Nebuchadnezzar's image of gold, when they boldly said to the king,

> If we are thrown into the blazing furnace, the God we serve is able to save us from it, and he will rescue us from your hand, O king. But even if he does not, we want you to know, O king, that we will not serve your gods or worship the image of gold you have set up. (Daniel 3:17-18)

This passage shows us three levels of faith. The first level is the statement "Our God is able to deliver us." All believers will testify to the fact that God is able. We do not have a problem with the first level. The second level is the statement "He will rescue us from your hand." Because we have a faith history of being blessed and delivered by God, we are not troubled by the second level. However, the third level, which states, "But even if he does not . . . ," gives us difficulties because when we are confronted with this third level, we must exercise our faith not in order to be kept from a problem, but in order to remain in and make it through a difficult situation.

Here, God exercises a different form of deliverance. It requires that we experience what we would rather not go through. Yet, it takes us to a level of faith that makes us stronger because it acknowledges the work of God in whatever situation we find ourselves. The prophet Habakkuk said,

"Though the fig tree does not bud and there are no grapes on the vines, though the olive crop fails and the fields produce no food, though there are no sheep in the pen and no cattle in the stalls, yet I will rejoice in the LORD, I will be joyful in God my Savior" (Habakkuk 3:17-18). Such a position of faith will never be defeated or disappointed, because God's will can be discovered in the easy or the difficult, the beautiful or the ugly, the good or the bad.

New Testament Examples of Faith

Faith is an incredible medium through which we can know or discern God's will. Someone has said, "Faith is not about us getting our way with God; it is about God getting his way with us."

The Canaanite Woman

The story of the Canaanite woman is an excellent model for interpreting the will of God. She believed that a persistent faith was more powerful than an inactive faith. We must do more than just claim to have faith; we must persist in the exercise of our faith in order to discover God's will.

> Leaving that place, Jesus withdrew to the region of Tyre and Sidon. A Canaanite woman from that vicinity came to him, crying out, "Lord, Son of David, have mercy on me! My daughter is suffering terribly from demon-possession." Jesus did not answer a word. So his disciples came to him and urged him, "Send her away, for she keeps crying out after us." He answered, "I was sent only to the lost sheep of Israel." The woman came and knelt before him. "Lord, help me!" she said. He replied, "It is not right to take the children's bread and toss it to their dogs." "Yes, Lord," she said, "but even the dogs eat the crumbs that fall from their masters' table." Then Jesus answered, "Woman, you have great faith! Your request is granted." And her daughter was healed from that very hour. (Matthew 15:21-28)

Notice the woman's actions and attitudes in her encounter with Jesus: (1) she came boldly to Jesus; (2) she endured insults; (3) she worshiped Jesus; (4) she was persistent; and (5) she was humble (having been brought so low that nothing that anyone else said mattered).

In the resolution to this encounter, we find that the faith of the Canaanite woman made her "hang in there" until God's will was made known in the life of her daughter. She refused to let public opinion and prejudice keep her from her blessing. In fact, the woman was willing to settle for crumbs. And her faith was rewarded: Jesus healed the child through the intercession of the mother. Jesus did not meet the daughter, but the daughter was healed after the mother met Jesus.

The *intentional will* of God was that this woman have her anxiety mitigated and her daughter healed. The *circumstantial will* of God was manifested in the woman's daughter being demon-possessed. Because of this circumstance, God's *intentional will* was not immediately disclosed. However, the *ultimate will* of God was that this woman be granted healing for her daughter. She had great faith!

The Centurion's Servant

> When Jesus had entered Capernaum, a centurion came to him, asking for help. "Lord," he said, "my servant lies at home paralyzed and in terrible suffering." Jesus said to him, "I will go and heal him." The centurion replied, "Lord, I do not deserve to have you come under my roof. But just say the word, and my servant will be healed." . . . When Jesus heard this, he was astonished and said to those following him, "I tell you the truth, I have not found anyone in Israel with such great faith." (Matthew 8:5-8,10)

This passage is particularly amazing because here is a pagan, a representative of the oppressive Roman government, who moves to the head of the class of faith. The passage says nothing about the servant's faith; nor does it deal with the future commitment of the centurion or his servant to Jesus. However, the centurion was able to discover God's will in that particular situation. "Then Jesus said to the centurion, 'Go! It will be done just as you believed it would.' And his servant was healed at that very hour" (Matthew 8:13).

Here, *the intentional will* of God was that the centurion's servant be healed and that both the centurion and the servant have an encounter with the Eternal One. The *circumstantial will* was manifested in the many things that had to be overcome in order to discover God's will: paganism, Roman oppression, pride, and arrogance. However, God's *ultimate will* was not necessarily accomplished in the text because we don't know if either the servant or the centurion ever acknowledged Jesus as Savior.

God Is Sovereign

By faith, the walls of Jericho fell, after the people had marched around them for seven days. By faith the prostitute Rahab, because she welcomed the spies, was not killed with those who were disobedient. . . . Gideon, Barak, Samson, Jephthah, David, Samuel and the prophets . . . through faith conquered kingdoms, administered justice, and gained what was promised. . . . Others were tortured and refused to be released, so that they might gain a better resurrection. Some faced jeers and flogging, while still others were chained and put in prison. . . . These were all commended for their faith, yet none of them received what had been promised. (Hebrews 11:30-33,35-36,39)

From this Scripture, we could conclude either that God is good or that God is evil. We might wonder why some were delivered miraculously and others were killed for the faith. Once again, this passage is definitive in declaring that Jesus is Lord of both miracle and mutilation. Unless we embrace these twins, we will forever be on the brink of deserting the ranks of the faithful. When we speak of interpreting God's will through faith, we must never forget that God is sovereign. What does it mean to say that God is sovereign? It is God's prerogative to do as he wills in each of our lives. The sovereignty of God means that there are no shocks or surprises where God is concerned. A tragedy or a calamity is just another piece of the puzzle that needs to come together.

Whether we are delivered miraculously or whether we suffer along the way, eventually we all end up together in death.

For those who are not delivered, God's *intentional will* is that we bring glory to him. Suffering, which is permitted under God's *circumstantial will,* is also designed to bring God glory. Finally, then, we will spend eternity with God, which, above all else, brings glory to God.

The Increase of Our Faith

After a teaching from Jesus on the challenge of forgiveness, the apostles said to him, "Increase our faith!" (Luke 17:5). No matter how strong our faith may be, there is always room for an increase. There is no room for spiritual pride. Faith is an essential ingredient for interpreting the will of God. But our faith must be in God rather than in our selfish goals. Such a faith grows and expands because it is focused on pleasing God rather than us. How does our faith grow? Faith grows through disappointment. Sometimes, we get a better glimpse of God's will when we are disappointed. Since we operate under a benevolent providence, "we know that in all things God works for the good of those who love him" (Romans 8:28). Faith also grows through victories. What God has already done strengthens us for blessings still on the horizon. In addition, faith grows through a serious and systematic study of the word of God. The apostle Paul assures us that "faith comes from hearing the message, and the message is heard through the word of Christ" (Romans 10:17).

Perhaps most important, faith grows through what Danish theologian Søren Kierkegaard (1813–55) calls a "leap of faith," where no matter the situation or circumstance, we always leap from the dark into the light. The two criminals crucified with Jesus offer a striking example of discovering God's will even in a most trying situation. One hurled verbal abuse at Jesus, taunting him to save all three of them. The other said to his fellow criminal,

> "Don't you fear God . . . since you are under the same sentence? We are punished justly, for we are getting what our deeds deserve. But this man has done nothing wrong." Then he said to

Jesus, "Remember me when you come into your kingdom," and Jesus replied, "I tell you the truth, today you will be with me in paradise." (Luke 23:40-43)

What an amazing leap of faith! This man found God's will for his fleeting life and for eternity. In spite of his felonious behavior, by faith he was able to see Jesus through sin, suffering, selfishness, and scorn. By taking a leap of faith, he discovered God's *intentional will,* which was that he live in accordance with the will of God. Under God's *circumstantial will,* he had committed himself to a life of crime, and thus God's *intentional will* was put on hold. But because he took a leap of faith, he intersected with the *ultimate will* of God, which was that he be eternally with Jesus in paradise.

CHAPTER 8

Fellowship with God

IT IS TRUE THAT WE ARE ABLE TO DISCERN THE DIVINE WILL AS we spend time with God. This can take the forms of a personal relationship, meditation on the word of God, fasting, and prayer. Quite simply, the more time you spend with God, the better able you are to understand God.

A Personal Relationship with God

The Bible is key to understanding the will of God. Without the written revelation, we would be like a rudderless ship. The word of God helps us to answer or respond to questions such as "Whom should I marry?" and "Which job offer should I accept?" Our relationship with God as it intersects with his Word is indispensable for interpreting the will of God. In our intimate relationship with God, we are better able to discern the divine will for our lives. Jesus gives us insight into the divine will and our relationship with God the Father as his friends.

"I no longer call you servants, because a servant does not know his master's business. Instead, I have called you friends, for everything that I learned from my Father I have made known to you" (John 15:15).

Jesus describes a relationship elevated, from servants to friends, which means deeper and better insight into his will. Because his disciples are his friends, they are privy to an understanding that others do not have, not because they are superior, but because he has made it known to them.

Moses also was singled out as a friend of the Lord: "The LORD would speak to Moses face to face, as a man speaks with his friend" (Exodus 33:11). And Abraham's intimate relationship with God is highlighted in 2 Chronicles 20:7, where Jehoshaphat, praying to God, refers to "Abraham your friend." Abraham's continual fellowship with God imbued him with the initiative to move out in search of God's will.

Abraham provides a wonderful example of divine-human intimacy when he seeks to find a wife for his son Isaac from his native land of Mesopotamia. Abraham did not have the benefit of written revelation, but nonetheless he was the beneficiary of a personal relationship with God. (This personal relationship became the foundation for the written revelation.) Even though God communicated with and made revelations to Abraham many times, Abraham did not perfectly understand God's will, and neither will we. There will always be pockets of doubt as we struggle to know and to do God's will. This can be seen clearly from the following passage, which depicts Abraham's desire for Isaac to have a wife.

> Abraham was now old and well advanced in years, and the LORD had blessed him in every way. He said to the chief servant in his household, . . . "I want you to swear by the LORD, the God of heaven and the God of earth, that you will not get a wife for my son from the daughters of the Canaanites, among whom I am living, but will go to my country and my own relatives and get a wife for my son Isaac." (Genesis 24:1-4)

Through its description of the servant's journey to Mesopotamia to find a wife for Isaac and the success of this endeavor, Genesis 24 gives us insights into the process of discovering the will of God.

- A human desire is established (Abraham wants Isaac to have a wife).

- God does not hold the human will captive (the servant acknowledges that the woman he selects may be unwilling to return with him).

- God guides and prods people, but does not control them (God's angel accompanies the servant).

- We should consult God for guidance and direction through prayer (the servant prays).

- Human desire is not necessarily contrary to the will of God (the servant's request for a specific sign is answered).

- When wills come together without prior knowledge or consultation, we may conclude that God may be at work (the servant's wish and Rebekah's actions coincide, even though they had never met).

- When God moves, we should honor God through worship (the servant worships).

- God leads us (Rebekah and her relatives see God's hand in the sign).

- Even after divine signs have been given, human nature may still hesitate (Rebekah's relatives want to detain her from going with the servant).

- What we want always has the potential for circumventing what God has intended (Rebekah could have refused to return with the servant).

- We must choose to follow God's will (Rebekah, though free to decline, consents to the marriage).

Finally, these components fall into place when Isaac meets and marries Rebekah. This brings the divine will, through God's friend Abraham, to fulfillment.

Meditating on the Word

Meditating on God's word brings success if we practice what we have learned. God's will is discovered when we activate our faith. "Do not let this Book of the Law depart from your mouth; meditate on it day and night, so that you may be careful to do everything written in it. Then you will be prosperous and successful" (Joshua 1:8).

Through meditating on God's law, the psalmist discovered God's will for his public and private life as it affects what he listens to, how he lives, and what he does.

> Blessed is the man who does not walk in the counsel of the wicked or stand in the way of sinners or sit in the seat of mockers. But his delight is in the law of the LORD, and on his law he meditates day and night. He is like a tree planted by streams of water, which yields its fruit in season and whose leaf does not wither. Whatever he does prospers. (Psalm 1:1-3)

Meditating on the written revelation—the Bible—cannot and must not be divorced from one's personal walk with God. For faith to be authentic, these two must go hand in hand. The will of God is more easily discerned when we have perpetual fellowship with him. The Scripture says, "Enoch walked with God" (Genesis 5:22). This is testimony to Enoch's consistent fellowship with God. When it came time for Enoch to depart this life, he felt at ease to go on and be with God forever. Because of his daily walk, he did not struggle when God took him. Rather, Enoch's will was at peace with God's will.

Fasting

The purpose of fasting is to subordinate the flesh to the spirit so that we may align ourselves with the will of God. It is powerful for discerning God's will in the midst of a number of different circumstances, including national disaster.

> Then David and all the men with him took hold of their clothes and tore them. They mourned and wept and fasted till evening for

> Saul and his son Jonathan, and for the army of the LORD and the house of Israel, because they had fallen by the sword. (2 Samuel 1:11-12)

Even though Saul was David's aggressive enemy, David loved him and his son Jonathan. David and the men with him fasted in sadness, but also in submission to the *circumstantial will* of God. It was not God's *intentional will* that Saul would die under such circumstances, but when he departed from God's will through disobedience, the circumstances kicked in, and God's *ultimate will* was done: Saul was eliminated from a position that God never wanted Israel to have, and David became king in his stead.

Fasting can also be effective in the discovery of God's will in personal tragedy.

> The LORD struck the child that Uriah's wife had borne to David, and he became ill. David pleaded with God for the child. He fasted and went into his house and spent the nights lying on the ground . . . . On the seventh day, the child died. (2 Samuel 12:15-16,18a)

Fasting is not a magic wand that gives success in all situations. Fasting opens the door for a deeper fellowship with God that enables us to discern the divine will and accept the reality of a situation. In spite of David's fasting and hoping that his child would live, the child died. The child was not going to be resuscitated. This does not mean that David's effort was totally for naught, for he was strengthened by fasting. Fasting enabled David to get up and go on with his life; he could pick up the pieces and move on.

Fasting heightens our fellowship with God and strengthens us in the face of overwhelming odds. In 2 Chronicles 20:1-3, we read,

> The Moabites and the Ammonites with some of the Meunites came to make war on Jehoshaphat. Some men came and told Jehoshaphat. . . . Alarmed, Jehoshaphat resolved to inquire of the LORD, and he proclaimed a fast for all Judah.

Jehoshaphat was one of Judah's greatest kings. He had fellowship with God and followed in God's ways prior to his moment of fear. However, in spite of his fear, he still discovered God's will for his people through fasting. So in his case, fellowship with God plus fasting translated into victory over Judah's enemies.

Ezra is another good example of someone who discovered God's will through fasting. Because Ezra was already on speaking terms with God, fasting prepared him to find an answer for his petition to God for a safe passage for the families returning to Jerusalem from captivity (Ezra 8:21-23).

During the Persian captivity, Nehemiah discovered God's will through fasting. Because of his concern for the destruction of Jerusalem, Nehemiah sought God's will in terms of what he could do to lead the returning exiles in rebuilding Jerusalem (Nehemiah 1:1-4).

Queen Esther employed fasting as a means of securing God's liberating power in the salvation of her people. Through fasting, the nation's mind was focused on a God who can deliver in spite of that nation's sin. Fasting also emboldened Esther to break a cultural prohibition against entering the king's presence without permission in order for God's will to be established through her husband, who was the king of Persia.

> Then Esther sent this reply to Mordecai: "Go, gather together all the Jews who are in Susa, and fast for me. Do not eat or drink for three days, night or day. I and my maids will fast as you do. When this is done, I will go to the king, even though it is against the law. And if I perish, I perish." (Esther 4:15-16)

As a result of this period of fellowship through fasting, God's final will was established. The whole exiled nation was delivered, and the festival of Purim was instituted.

Fasting was also a powerful weapon in Jesus' spiritual arsenal as he sought to know and to do his Father's will. It is strategic that Jesus fasted after his baptism and before he began his public ministry. Fasting was not a ritual for Jesus; it was a sign of perpetual fellowship between him and his Father. During his temptation in the desert (Matthew 4:1-11), Jesus was empowered to know and to do God's will. It is an ongoing moral imperative that we know what to do and how to behave in every situation. For Jesus, the Scriptures formed the basis for his morality. Because he walked day by day with his Father, and because he knew the Scriptures, he had a deeper insight into the will of God and could answer the tempter at every turn: "Man does not live on bread alone, but on every word that comes from the mouth of God." "Do not put the Lord your God to the test." "Worship the Lord your God, and serve him only."

In the early church, fasting in a context of worship opened the door for the church at Antioch to discover God's will regarding missions and evangelism. The Holy Spirit spoke after the church had fasted. The church prayed and laid hands on Barnabas and Paul after fasting for an extended period of time (Acts 13:1-3). As a result, the first missionary journey in church history was launched.

Prayer

It is a given in the community of faith that prayer is a powerful and an indispensable resource for discovering the will of God. It has been said that the purpose of prayer is not to get humanity's will done in heaven but to get God's will done on earth. Prayer is not about twisting God's arm in order to have our way; it is about discovering and surrendering to God's will. Unless we are the epitome of arrogance, we will confess that no one knows the will of God perfectly as it intersects all human situations. However, we continue to pray because we must. Persistence in prayer is a key to understanding the will of God. The fact that we have not been answered clearly is no reason to give up. It has been said that sometimes the darkest time of the night is just before the dawn. Therefore, we must keep on praying.

> Then Jesus told his disciples a parable to show them that they should always pray and not give up. He said: "In a certain town there was a judge who neither feared God nor cared about men. And there was a widow in that town who kept coming to him with the plea, 'Grant me justice against my adversary.' For some time

he refused. But finally he said to himself, 'Even though I don't fear God or care about men, yet because this widow keeps bothering me, I will see that she gets justice, so that she won't eventually wear me out with her coming!'" (Luke 18:1-5)

In this passage, we can clearly see that the will of even an unjust and uncaring judge is discovered through persistence. How much more confident may we be that prayerful persistence will reveal the will of our loving and just God!

Prayer does not always exempt us from potentially harmful situations. Jesus spent all night in prayer and still picked fickle disciples, including Judas Iscariot, who became a traitor. In spite of Jesus' choice of the twelve disciples with all their failings and shortcomings, God's will still was done. Jesus sought to discover his Father's will through trusting obedience in the garden of Gethsemane (Matthew 26:36-46). God's will for us, even as it was for Jesus, is not always clear. We exaggerate to our own dishonor when we claim to understand God's will perfectly. Prayer is not a magic wand that can dissolve our human limitations. Even if we deny this reality, the truth still stares us in the face. When Jesus submitted to his Father's will, he found peace. Prayer is about our will in search of God's will. Once our will runs into God's will, then our will is destroyed in the collision. It is then that we pray, "Let my will be lost in thine."

In our day of "Disneyland Christianity," we are mocked and held hostage to a sick theology that teaches us that God will do anything we ask. This ultimately leads to disappointment and disillusionment as we pray for carnal things. Jesus prayed for his cup of suffering to be removed, but finally submitted his will to God's, and received a cross.

Again, it is not always easy to discern or to know the will of God. However, there is one thing we can be certain of: God cannot be manipulated into acting according to our own selfish agendas. Because we have insight into the nature of God, we can speak with relative certainty about God's *intentional will* and God's *ultimate will.* But because of things that arise under God's *circumstantial will,* we are often confounded when God allows certain things to happen. The Epistle of James extends this discussion further:

> You want something but don't get it. You kill and covet, but you cannot have what you want. You quarrel and fight. You do not have, because you do not ask God. When you ask, you do not receive, because you ask with wrong motives, that you may spend what you get on your pleasures. (James 4:2-3)

Clearly, then, if we pray with wrong motives, we will be constantly confused in trying to determine the will of God. Only when we pray for those things that bring God glory can we find peace.

Sometimes God's will is discovered through an affirmative answer to prayer. "So Peter was kept in prison, but the church was earnestly praying to God for him" (Acts 12:5). A few verses later, we see Peter being delivered miraculously from prison. This must be juxtaposed with James the brother of John, who was beheaded. Did James pray? Why was he not delivered? The answer is that both men actually were delivered, because Jesus is Lord of both triumph and tragedy.

King Hezekiah's prayer was answered in the affirmative after he was told by the prophet Isaiah that death was imminent. The Lord added fifteen years to his life (Isaiah 38:1-5). Even though his petition was granted, it was only the postponement of the inevitable. Many would argue that if he had died, Judah would have been spared its darkest hour because his evil son Manasseh would not have been born. In spite of Hezekiah's circumstances, he found God's will through prayer. Notice that God's answer came with a note of tenure: on the sixteenth year, Hezekiah would die. So sometimes both dread and destiny are tied together as we pray to know God's will.

As we seek to know God's will through prayer, we sometimes do not know what we should pray for. I was driving the late George Buttrick to see his wife, who was in a convalescent facility in Louisville, Kentucky, and who, sadly, often could not recognize either of us. I asked him, "Doctor, what do we pray for now?" He replied, "Mack, I don't know what I ought to pray for. I am tempted to pray that God would turn the clock back to our wedding day and give us another sixty-three years of bliss. But God is not stupid and neither am I. So, I just pray and trust God."

Sometimes, as we pray to know God's will, we are kept from, or within, situations and circumstances. Shadrach, Meshach, and Abednego were not kept *from* the fire but *in* the fire. It was then that they found the overwhelming presence of the Eternal One.

> Then Nebuchadnezzar was furious with Shadrach, Meshach and Abednego, and his attitude toward them changed. He ordered the furnace heated seven times hotter then usual. . . . So these men, wearing their robes, trousers, turbans and other clothes, were bound and thrown into the blazing furnace. . . . Then King Nebuchadnezzar leaped to his feet in amazement and asked his advisers, "Weren't there three men that we tied up and threw into the fire?" They replied, "Certainly, O king." He said, "Look! I see four men walking around in the fire, unbound and unharmed, and the fourth looks like a son of the gods." (Daniel 3:19,21,24-25)

Although the three Hebrews gave no public demonstration of prayer at this time, it stands to reason that because of their faith, they lived in an attitude of prayer. Here, God's will is seen clearly. God's *intentional will* was that they would not be destroyed by the king of Babylon. However, because of the events of the fiery furnace that took place under God's *circumstantial will,* they faced the potential of being exterminated. But finally, they were delivered unharmed, and God's *ultimate will* was established.

In 1980, I received an invitation to become copastor of Mount Olive Baptist Church in Fort Lauderdale, Florida, then under the pastorate of George E. Weaver. After saying no, I was prompted in my spirit to pray for knowledge of God's will. At the time, I was senior pastor of Green Castle Baptist Church in Prospect, Kentucky, and visiting professor at Simmons Bible College and Southern Baptist Theological Seminary.

The issues seemed to be clear, but still I needed to discover God's will for my ministry. By staying near Louisville, Kentucky, I could continue my visiting professorships as well as remain senior pastor of Green Castle Baptist Church. At that time, Florida had no accredited theological seminary. Also, Green Castle was a much smaller congregation of about three hundred members, while Mount Olive's parishioners numbered around twenty-eight hundred. Neither money nor fame nor a promotion was my object. But if I went to Mount Olive, my future was uncertain because my succeeding George Weaver was not going to be automatic. This uncertainty drove my wife up a wall. Therefore, her reluctance in coming made my decision more difficult. Beyond this, I wondered whether Dr. Weaver and I would collide theologically. So, I prayed to know God's will.

I flew down to preach on a Sunday and stayed overnight to teach a Monday night Bible class. When Dr. Weaver raised his hand to ask a question, I suspected that perhaps I had contradicted his theological belief. He immediately got up and confirmed my suspicions, but then he said, "Dr. Carter is right in what he has said. I had another viewpoint, but his viewpoint is crystal clear. This is why God told me to invite Dr. Carter to be my copastor. This is God's choice, even though he has not agreed to come." Driving from the church that night, we stopped at a traffic light, and the Lord said, "It's all right to come." It was then that I knew that I was in the will of the Lord.

We moved to Fort Lauderdale in August of 1981 for me to become copastor of Mount Olive. Upon Dr. Weaver's retirement in November of 1982, the church voted unanimously for me to succeed him as senior pastor. Through persistence in prayer, I have been at the helm of this great church for almost two decades. I am absolutely certain that I am where I am supposed to be because I prayed to know God's will.

CHAPTER 9

Discussion

OFTEN, THE INSIGHTS OF OTHERS CAN DISCLOSE GOD'S WILL. The adage is true: "Two heads are better than one." No one is infallible in interpreting God's will. Therefore, we must be open to the insights of others. The seven ecumenical church councils held between 325 and 787 are evidence of the need for lengthy and wide-ranging discussion of God's purposes—no one theologian had all the answers. In the early church in Jerusalem, the apostles knew the power of discussion. Discussion is necessary because others—teachers, pastors, poets, plumbers, parents, physicians—have had kindred experiences. Because others have traveled this way before, we can get help with the challenges along our path.

Discussion and Vocational Decisions

We must not be left alone to make major decisions. Before I enrolled in seminary, I discussed the significance of this decision with several ministers, including Charles Pinkney Brown, Lewis Napoleon Anderson, Oliver Van Pinkston, Alfred Deter Lonon (my own pastor), and George Edward Weaver (my immediate predecessor in my current pastorate). All of these great men of God gave me wise counsel that has blessed my life immeasurably. Through their counsel, I know beyond a shadow of a doubt that their advice was God-inspired.

Before I spoke with these giants in the faith, I attempted to circumvent seminary and get a master's degree in religion from Stetson University in Deland, Florida. In the early 1970s, there was no accredited theological seminary in Florida. The closest one would have been either in Atlanta or in New Orleans. At the time, I did not want to leave the Saint John Baptist Church of Ocala, Florida, because it was a growing church and held great promise. So, I visited the Stetson campus with the expectation of enrolling in the university. I met with the head of the department of religion. He greeted me cordially, but, after perusing my transcript, he strongly discouraged me from attending Stetson. He said that in light of the fact that not many African American pastors in the country at that time had accredited seminary degrees, he would recommend that I attend seminary. All sorts of thoughts raced through my mind. Even though the university was by that time fully integrated, I believed that the same old racial bias was being used to discourage and exclude me. I felt insulted and demeaned. Even though he said that my transcript showed that I had a brilliant mind, I was convinced that he did not want me at that university.

It was then that I discussed the matter with the ministers whom I mentioned. Because of my discussions with the university department head and my colleagues, I resigned my pastorate and enrolled full-time in seminary in Louisville, Kentucky. By discussing the matter with others, I was able to make one of the most important decisions in my life. That experience has opened doors for me across the world. I know without a doubt that I was, and am, in the will of God.

Discussion and Administrative Decisions

The story of Moses and his father-in-law, Jethro, in Exodus 18 is a wonderful example of interpreting God's will through discussion.

The next day Moses took his seat to serve as judge for the people, and they stood around him from morning till evening. When his father-in-law saw all that Moses was doing for the people, he said, "What is this you are doing for the people? Why do you alone sit as judge, while all these people stand around you from morning till evening?" Moses answered him, "Because the people come to me to seek God's will. Whenever they have a dispute, it is brought to me, and I decide between the parties and inform them of God's decrees and laws." (Exodus 18:13-16)

Upon hearing this, Jethro proceeded to tell Moses that he would wear himself out if he kept up that routine. Jethro advised Moses to divide the responsibility of judging between others whom he should select, putting them in charge over groups ranging in size from tens to thousands. These "under-judges" would hear the simple cases, and bring the difficult cases to Moses. Jethro concluded, "If you do this and God so commands, you will be able to stand the strain, and all these people will go home satisfied" (Exodus 18:23).

From this model, we can see clearly that not only did the people discover God's will through Moses, but also, Moses discovered God's will through discussing the matter with Jethro. It was God's will for Moses to judge the people, but it was not God's will for him to destroy himself in the process. The modern-day church pastor (or other leader) can still drink from Jethro's fountain of wisdom. If we continue to heed the advice of Jethro, we will have strong pastors and powerful churches.

Discussion and Majority Rule

We must always seek to know and to do God's will rather than our own. Many people have gone down the path to destruction thinking that they knew the will of God, only to be defeated because of the absence of discussion and feedback. But although discussion is necessary, it can backfire if we do not engage the right ears. Such was the case when King Ahab of Israel asked King Jehoshaphat of Judah to join him in recapturing the land of Ramoth Gilead from the king of Aram. Jehoshaphat agreed, but he added a request.

> Jehoshaphat . . . said to the king of Israel, "First seek the counsel of the LORD." So the king of Israel brought together the prophets—about four hundred men—and asked them, "Shall I go to war against Ramoth Gilead, or shall I refrain?" "Go," they answered, "for the LORD will give it into the king's hand." But Jehoshaphat asked, "Is there not a prophet of the LORD here whom we can inquire of?" (1 Kings 22:5-7)

Even though the discussion between Ahab and Jehoshaphat was fruitful, Jehoshaphat felt the need to discover God's will. This discussion was further complicated by four hundred false prophets giving consent. Now that they had a majority, perhaps unanimous, opinion favoring the attack, must it reflect the will of God? We must be careful not to automatically equate God's will with the majority. A majority of the people called for the crucifixion of the Carpenter from Nazareth. Even though the discussion with Ahab plus the affirmation from the four hundred prophets would have been enough to seal any decision, Jehoshaphat, being more spiritually sensitive than Ahab, called for a further polling of the house. He probably was wondering how anyone could get that many preachers together and have them all agree on the same thing! So, another prophet, Micaiah son of Imlah, was summoned and questioned. Although Micaiah was just one prophet, and an unpopular one at that, through him Ahab was to discover the *ultimate will* of God for his life: defeat and death. In the end, only God's will matters.

Discussion and Difficult Situations

The story of the Moabites and the Ammonites coming to do battle with Judah during the reign of King Jehoshaphat is a great example of the need for discussion in order to discover God's will in difficult times (2 Chronicles 20:1-30). Although his nerves were on edge and his adrenaline was flowing like a river, Jehoshaphat had the wisdom not to act in haste or make a decision based on fear. He discussed the matter. First, he consulted God. Second, he called the people together to inform them of the crisis at hand. Third, he listened to the voice of Jahaziel the Levite, as he was led by the spirit. As a result, God's will was declared and discovered. We must never forget that the Holy Spirit is available and more than able to lead us into God's will.

Or consider this passage from Jeremiah.

> Then the word of the LORD came to Jeremiah the prophet: "This is what the LORD, the God of Israel, says: Tell the king of Judah, who sent you to inquire of me, 'Pharaoh's army, which has marched out to support you, will go back to its own land, to Egypt. Then the Babylonians will return and attack this city; they will capture it and burn it down.'" (Jeremiah 37:6-8)

The discovery of God's will is not always a pleasant affair. It was not God's *intentional will* that Judah go into captivity. But because they insisted on living outside of his the divine will, God's *circumstantial will* kicked in, and the nation of Judah was facing oppression. King Zedekiah was apprised in advance of what was going to happen, but he never repented. Foolishly, he believed that somehow God would relent without repentance on the part of the people. It was in this context that Zedekiah asked the prophet Jeremiah, "Is there any word from the LORD?" Jeremiah answered, "Yes, you will be handed over to the king of Babylon" (Jeremiah 37:17). Even though Zedekiah discussed the matter with the prophet, because of the nation's arrogance in regard to repentance, God's *circumstantial will* produced a seventy-year captivity. The whole country became desolate, and the people served the king of Babylon for seventy years. If you live outside of God's will, you will be judged.

Discussion and Choosing Church Leaders

The matter of searching for God's will with regard to church leadership calls for collaborative effort. After the ascension of Jesus, the church made a move to replace Judas, who had committed suicide. The disciples of Jesus struggled to know

God's will in regard to a replacement for Judas (Acts 1:21). Much wisdom can be transmitted through discussion. Even though they were saddened by the tragic end of Judas, they were overwhelmingly strengthened by their resurrected Lord. It was in this light that the disciples sought to know God's will. Through discussion, they reached a resolution of what to do:

> So they proposed two men: Joseph called Barsabbas (also known as Justus) and Matthias. Then they prayed, "Lord, you know everyone's heart. Show us which of these two you have chosen to take over this apostolic ministry, which Judas left to go where he belongs." Then they cast lots, and the lot fell to Matthias; so he was added to the eleven apostles. (Acts 1:23-26)

Another example is found in Acts 6:1-8. Many commentators reject the notion that this Scripture highlights the origin of the office of the deacon. No matter where one stands on that issue, we can all agree that the early church was seeking God's will collaboratively as well as individually. When a problem arose regarding the fair distribution of food among the Greek and Jewish widows,

> the Twelve gathered all the disciples together and said, "It would not be right for us to neglect the ministry of the word of God in order to wait on tables. Brothers, choose seven men from among you who are known to be full of the Spirit and wisdom. We will turn this responsibility over to them and will give our attention to prayer and the ministry of the word."

And so it was done. God's will was expressed through a resolution of the conflict, and their decision would be confirmed through the miracles that the Twelve performed and the power of their evangelism.

CHAPTER 10

Common Sense

IT IS EASY TO SPEAK ABOUT USING COMMON SENSE, BUT TO understand what that means is much more difficult. Common sense is more than intuition or having a hunch. It is about making decisions based upon what we know about God, history, culture, Scripture, and our own experiences. Common sense is not a casual guess at what we should do. It is about making a decision based upon our understanding of God's will. Therefore, we must make a clear distinction between the intentional, circumstantial, and ultimate wills of God. To do less is to court disaster, fanaticism, cynicism, and a toxic faith. Common sense is not the ultimate in understanding God's will, but it can be "a very present help in time of trouble."

On the other hand, what we call common sense can keep us from attempting great things. Abraham, in Genesis 22:1-18, is a marvelous example of someone who became heroic because he defied the usual definition of common sense. God tested Abraham by commanding him to build an altar and sacrifice his son Isaac. Just as Abraham was raising the knife over Isaac, the Lord's angel commanded him to stop. Clearly, the world would not have been the same if Abraham had used common sense as it is usually defined. His gesture was based upon his relationship with God.

Moses is another example of someone who defied the canon of logic as he sought to do the will of God.

> The LORD said, "I have indeed seen the misery of my people in Egypt. I have heard them crying out because of their slave drivers, and I am concerned about their suffering. . . . So now, go. I am sending you to Pharaoh to bring my people the Israelites out of Egypt." (Exodus 3:7,10)

Sending Moses (even if accompanied by Aaron) to face down the pharaoh, the most powerful man in the world, did not make good sense. However, Moses, equipped by God for this seemingly hopeless task, was able to make the right decision.

Similarly, Queen Esther refused to allow a definition of fear to keep her from achieving greatness as she discovered her destiny in the will of God. Torn between personal and national destiny, she was able to make the right decision. Many times, what we want to do personally gets in the way of what needs to be done for the group. While Esther served as the queen of Persia, a plot was underway to exterminate the Jewish people—her people. What we call common sense would dictate that she stay out of the way and look out for herself. Forget the nation! But her cousin Mordecai served as a source of faith history that allowed her to use common sense in discovering God's will. Mordecai told her,

> Do not think that because you are in the king's house you alone of all the Jews will escape. For if you remain silent at this time, relief and deliverance for the Jews will arise from another place, but you and your father's family will perish. And who knows but that you have come to royal position for such a time as this? (Esther 4:13-14).

Esther took action, and she discovered God's will for herself and her people, which was that they be spared. As a result of Esther's bold action, the festival of Purim came to be, and is still observed by Jews today.

Or consider Jesus' disciples sailing on the Sea of Galilee the day Peter got out of the boat to walk on water. They must have thought him to be insane! Where was his common sense!

> During the fourth watch of the night Jesus went out to them, walking on the lake. When the disciples saw him walking on the lake, they were terrified. "It's a ghost," they said, and cried out in fear. But Jesus immediately said to them: "Take courage! It is I. Don't be afraid." "Lord, if it's you," Peter replied, "tell me to come to you on the water." "Come," he said. Then Peter got down out of the boat, walked on the water and came toward Jesus. (Matthew 14:25-29)

Peter, ignoring the laws of nature to heed the call of Jesus, heroically walked on water. He did not walk for long, but he did walk on water. This powerful moment of faith in the will of God, temporary though it may have been, crosses all boundaries of common sense. And as far as we know, no one else has won this battle with the waves, even momentarily.

When it comes to common sense and God's will, we must realize that this is a matter for believers to grapple with. Only believers would dare raise the question, "What is God's will for my life?" We raise the following questions as points of consideration and clarification.

Should Christians attempt strange things in order to prove our faith?

Most Christians (and probably all nonbelievers!) would agree that common sense dictates against playing tennis on a busy freeway. Because we have an understanding of God's nature and a knowledge of where tennis usually is played, we know that freeways were made not for tennis but for travel. There is nothing redemptive about playing tennis on a freeway. Nobody will be liberated. Therefore, we conclude that it would be a sign of insanity to do something so foolhardy. There is a difference between tempting God and trusting God.

It is not God's *intentional will* that we do anything that does not bring glory to God. This is why Jesus refused to heed the devil's taunts to jump off the pinnacle of the temple overlooking the Kidron Valley. There is a great distance between faith and presumption.

> Then the devil took him to the holy city and had him stand on the highest point of the temple. "If you are the Son of God," he said, "throw yourself down. For it is written: 'He will command his angels concerning you, and they will lift you up in their hands, so that you will not strike your foot against a stone.'" (Matthew 4:5-6)

It was not God's will for Jesus to put on a show in order to gain followers. How different Jesus was from the church in this new millennium! We pull out all kinds of heretical stops in order to get a crowd. After you jump off the pinnacle of the temple, what will be your next acrobatic challenge? Several years ago, a pastor announced that Michael Jackson would speak at his church the following Sunday. Many thought he was referring to the enormously popular musical entertainer. The next Sunday, neither the sanctuary nor the church grounds could accommodate the tremendous crowds. Reverend Michael Jackson did appear and preach the gospel, but the congregants left upset because they had come there to be entertained.

Musical entertainment is entertainment of a relatively harmless variety, but what of those who quote Scriptures about death-defying signs that prove the authenticity of the Christian faith?

> He said to them, "Go into all the world and preach the good news to all creation. Whoever believes and is baptized will be saved, but whoever does not believe will be condemned. And these signs will accompany those who believe: In my name they will drive out demons; they will speak in new tongues; they will pick up snakes with their hands; and when they drink deadly poison, it will not hurt them at all; they will place their hands on sick people, and they will get well." (Mark 16:15-18)

Most biblical scholars agree that Mark 16:9-20 is a later addition to that Gospel. The earliest manuscripts say that Mark's Gospel ends at 16:8. Whether verses 9-20 are authentic or not, most charismatic Christians would have no problem with new tongues, exorcisms, and the sick recovering; they just do not bother to drink poison and play with snakes. On the other hand, some zealous Christians practice these latter two as a test of their faith. Some have survived, barely, while others have died.

New Testament professor Frank Stagg believes that the practice of handling snakes grew out of Paul's experience on the island of Malta, where he was bitten by a viper—a venomous snake—and did not die (Acts 28:1-6). Without a doubt, healings, speaking in tongues, and exorcisms have been manifestations of the Spirit throughout church history. People have been delivered from snakebites and poisonous beverages, but such things should not be practiced on purpose.

Sometimes unthinking enthusiasm can lead to grave destruction. A young lady once told me that she had enough faith that if she stood in the middle of Interstate 95, cars and trucks would literally bounce off of her! Thank God she never tried it. Once again, there is a vast difference between trusting God and testing God. Let common sense—if you have it—serve you well.

Remember, we are justified by faith, not by snakes or (if God is gracious) surviving a speeding Mack truck. Daniel was placed in the lions' den, but after the first encounter, he did not see the need to make it a habit. So use common sense, and stay away from snakes, poison, and oncoming traffic. Toying with God tends to prove one's insanity rather than one's faith!

Now, some would argue along those lines that Dr. King was crazy for going to Memphis in 1968—that he didn't use the sense God gave him in avoiding a known risk. The first time he came, there was a disturbance, probably planned by FBI director J. Edgar Hoover. For his own safety, King left Memphis and returned to Atlanta. Several days later, he returned to Memphis, where he was assassinated on April 4, 1968. Did he use common sense? Was he in God's will? He was in Memphis seeking justice for sanitation workers. It is always God's will for us to seek to liberate those who are oppressed. It is not always in the kingdom's best interest for the believer to preserve his or her life. Sometimes, we are called to lose it in order to gain it. Like Paul on his way to Jerusalem, King was well aware of the danger that awaited him in Memphis. But because of whose he was, God's will was fulfilled in him in spite of danger and death. Common sense in service to the kingdom is more profound than self-preservation, and so, King was killed because he used uncommon sense.

Should I look to God to do for me what I should do for myself?

Simply to say, "I am waiting on God," has its merit, but when taken to the extreme, it leads to disappointment. God provides the conduit through which we are delivered, but we must take advantage of what God offers. As Christians, we must realize that "we are God's fellow workers" (1 Corinthians 3:9). The story is told of a religious fanatic who believed that he could stay at home and God would provide a turkey for him and his family for Christmas even though he had a hunting rifle to shoot one and a car to pick one up from the grocery store. He did neither, and no turkey was eaten in his house on Christmas Day. God will not allow us to presume in that fashion upon divine love and providence. It is common sense to do everything in our power to work with God.

Many overzealous Christians believe that going to a physician shows a lack of faith. But often there is confusion between faith and presumption. Authentic Christianity thanks God for pills *and* prayer. Both are in the will of God, and to choose between the two is to court disaster. There is no conflict between visiting a physician and offering a prayer of faith.

We must remember that Jesus never condemned anyone for going to a physician. Physicians are not God, but they are essential partners of God in the healing process. Jesus said, "It is not the healthy who need a doctor, but the sick"

(Matthew 9:12). Also, the apostle Paul kept Luke the physician with him not only as a spiritual confidant, but probably as his personal doctor too (2 Timothy 4:11).

Is it God's will for us to use any means necessary in order to be successful?

J. R. Ewing, a principal character on the television soap opera *Dallas,* said, "Once you give up on integrity, the rest of life is a piece of cake." The Christian, in order to intersect with the will of God, must always conduct himself or herself according to the principles of the kingdom of God. That is why it is arrogant and erroneous for America or any other nation to refer to itself as a Christian nation if it was formed by imperialism and is sustained by the evils of racism and materialism. To be a Christian nation is a radical notion, but it can be a reality only when the Carpenter of Nazareth's gospel is concretized. When that happens, the philosophy "by any means necessary" goes out the window.

To do anything you want in order to arrive where you are not supposed to be is to court disaster. Life is filled with those who have used any and all means to get to what is perceived as "the top." Once they are there, they discover that the pain of being out of God's will is too great to bear. Cassius and Brutus, coconspirators in the death of Julius Caesar, are tragic examples of those who used questionable means to get what they wanted. After the funeral oration, they too were killed. "Do not be deceived: God cannot be mocked. A man reaps what he sows" (Galatians 6:7). It is best to live our lives according to the tenets of the kingdom of God, which is to be in God's will.

If we accept that principle as a common sense guideline for pursuing and discerning God's will, then how do we answer the question about whether violence is an option for Christian behavior? How do we respond to the proliferation of nuclear weaponry worldwide, and particularly in our own nation?

Common sense that has been informed by Christian teachings would answer that violence is not an option for

Christian behavior. This sets the kingdom of God above all worldly systems. Although violence does occur within God's *circumstantial will,* it certainly is not God's *intentional will.* This is why war is such a dreadful thing. The prophet Isaiah had an exalted vision of nonaggression:

> He will judge between the nations and will settle disputes for many peoples. They will beat their swords into plowshares and their spears into pruning hooks. Nation will not take up sword against nation, nor will they train for war anymore. (Isaiah 2:4)

The prophet Zechariah also gives thumbs down to violence: "So [the angel] said to me, 'This is the word of the Lord to Zerubbabel: "Not by might nor by power, but by my Spirit," says the LORD Almighty'" (Zechariah 4:6).

Nuclear weapons represent the zenith in the evolution of sophisticated evil. Nothing that humankind has ever made equals them in terms of their ability to eradicate the human population. When scientific genius operates outside the spirit of Christ, one result is nuclear weapons. Because we know Jesus of Nazareth, who informs our commonsense decisions, we can conclude that nuclear weapons violate the *intentional will* of God.

Yet these are some of the circumstances that surround the existence of the bomb: the rise of Adolf Hitler and the onset of World War II; the fear of Hitler obtaining and using the bomb first; the fear of still others getting the bomb; and the illusion of the bomb as a deterrent in conjunction with the illusion that a nuclear war could be won.

Since nuclear weapons (not to mention chemical and biological weapons) are still with us, the church, by faith, must be the voice of Christ in the world, calling us away from the abyss of destruction. America and other nations have the power to destroy the whole world. When we consider the other nuclear powers in the world, we can clearly see the multiple possibilities for annihilation. But in spite of this, God's *ultimate will* has not yet been accomplished. Will we destroy ourselves? God gives us the common sense to say no.

Even apart from nuclear weaponry, violence in any form might destroy the enemy, but it destroys the aggressor much more. If the Christian church in America ever grasps this truth, it could lead a moral revolution in this country that would transform the world. While absolute pacifism might not be realistic in a sinful world, it is certain that in regard to violence, a more excellent way must be considered.

Jesus, our ultimate interpreter for this and all issues, has taught the church the futility of violence.

> Then the men stepped forward, seized Jesus and arrested him. With that, one of Jesus' companions reached for his sword, drew it out and struck the servant of the high priest, cutting off his ear. "Put your sword back in its place," Jesus said to him, "for all who draw the sword will die by the sword." (Matthew 26:50a-52)

Nobody wins if we live down to our lower selves. It is only when we take the path of creative nonviolence that we can claim the title "Christian."

Even after such horrifying events as the terrorist attacks on New York City and Washington D.C. on September 11, 2001, when thousands of innocent people die and the nation clamors for vengeance, the church must continue to seek God's will, faithfully and fearlessly. The real danger is that we may know the divine will—and refuse to conform to God's desires. Where should the church position itself in the wake of devastating national tragedy? We should be patriotic *and* prophetic, a difficult position to maintain when we encounter terrorism in our own neighborhoods and experience Jesus' Sermon on the Mount in our devotional reading. God's *ultimate will* is for peace and love to prevail, and so the church must always choose love over hate, even when bombs are falling.

What does common sense say about Christians and the common "vices" of alcohol consumption, tobacco use, overeating, gambling, etc.?

The Bible contains no blanket condemnation of drinking alcoholic beverages. In ancient times, wine was a common beverage, and it was also used medicinally (1 Timothy 5:23).

In ancient Israel, wine was safer to drink than water. Jesus himself drank wine, although not to excess. The apostle Paul calls for Christians to be filled with the Spirit rather than be filled with wine to the point of inebriation (Ephesians 5:18). Because of what can happen as a result of taking that first drink, I recommend abstinence as a discipline, but not as a direct command from God. Noah provides a poignant argument for the need for Christian abstinence from alcoholic beverages (Genesis 9:20-27). Common sense and personal experience should guide the responsible Christian in choices concerning alcohol consumption.

The Bible contains no prohibition against smoking or the use of tobacco products; it does not mention them at all. However, it does remind Christians that their body is the special residence of God. "Do you not know that your body is a temple of the Holy Spirit, who is in you, whom you have received from God? You are not your own; you were bought at a price. Therefore honor God with your body" (1 Corinthians 6:19-20).

By using tobacco products, common sense and the medical profession tell us that we jeopardize our own health and the health of others as well. This is further exacerbated by the use of celebrities to promote tobacco products. Because of this practice, many young people have been enticed and then hooked. More people die from tobacco products than from illicit drugs. This is not to say that drugs are less harmful than tobacco but to underline the seriousness of the dangers of tobacco use. It is my belief and counsel that neither tobacco nor illicit drugs should be used by believers.

The issue of gambling presents a dilemma comparable to alcohol consumption. The words "gamble" and "gambling" do not appear in the Bible, but the concept of casting lots does occur. Usually lots were cast to find out about a person, to divide lands, to choose a leader, to order and regulate the courses of people holding office, and to decide a controversy. So what we call gambling (which typically involves placing money on a risk) is neither condemned nor condoned by the Bible.

It is my conviction, however, that gambling should be condemned in the Spirit of Christ. Any practice is evil that exists for the purpose of disenfranchising many for the benefit of a few. Gambling gives a distorted view of reality that contradicts the will of God for our lives. It is not God's will that we win money at the expense of others, but it is God's will that we work for our living. Many individuals and families have been destroyed by gambling. Therefore, I believe the believer needs to avoid gambling at all costs.

And what about overeating—or what Scripture calls "gluttony"? We must be conscious of the fact that while millions of us eat so much, billions of others eat so little. Overeating causes many health problems, such as obesity, high blood pressure, heart disorders, diabetes, and kidney failure, all of which can lead to death. This alone should cause common sense to guide us in our eating habits. We must eat to live, not live to eat. The Christian must eat healthily for the sake of the kingdom. Self-control, temperance, and moderation are the behavioral patterns for all believers (Galatians 5:23).

• • •

Only when we live our lives in moderation, heeding the wisdom of common sense, can we know God's will more clearly. Invariably, the divine will is not in extremes, whether those extremes are overzealous demonstrations of faith, violent reactions to life's challenges and tragedies, or reckless immersion in addictive behaviors. As we go through life, energized by God's Word and the Holy Spirit, we can know and do God's will. "For in his will is our peace."

CONCLUSION

THE MUSINGS CONTAINED IN THESE PAGES HAVE IN NO WAY exhausted that which can be known about the will of God. However, I believe that what has been said here, whether you agree or disagree with the principles outlined, can be the beginning of a more profound discussion.

Talking about God is never easy, because the divine ways are so beyond our ways. "As high as the heavens are above the earth, so high are my ways and thoughts above yours," the Lord says (Isaiah 55:9). In this volume, I have tried to stay away from trivializing the mystery of God. God is God, and that divine reality defies any neat syllogism that conforms always to the canon of human logic. In this book I have also tried to avoid giving simple answers to difficult questions. While discussion is healthy, some things will remain inexplicable. In such cases, we must position ourselves with Ezekiel and declare, "Sovereign LORD, only you can answer that!" (Ezekiel 37:3).

In the wake of the terrorist attacks on America on September 11, 2001, we have been forced to wrestle in a profound way with critical theological issues. We have been compelled to forsake "bumper-sticker" Christianity and meaningless spiritual clichés. We have been required to define our terms in practical and concrete ways. Who is God? What is God like?

In such theological explorations, we must be open and kind in our dialogue about God, and we must also be specific about our own understanding of who God is. I am not a radical Christian fundamentalist, but it needs to be clearly established that the God of whom the Christian church speaks is the God who was incarnate in Jesus of Nazareth. We must be clear that Jesus of Nazareth is the ultimate interpreter of God's will for us.

We are humbled by the reality that no epistemological system is pervasive and comprehensive enough to understand the mind of God. God is greater than human intellect, greater than our powers of analysis. And, I would assert without hesitation, God is never threatened by our doubts nor by our denials. God desires us to use our minds in spite of the finitude of our human capacities.

It is my prayer that the skeptic who reads this book will be provoked to look a little deeper into the mystery that is God. May the young saint develop a more coherent language with which to dialogue about God's will, and may the mature believer discover incentive to expand his or her mind in pursuit of the mind of God. If, indeed, the reader of this book learns to talk about the will of God with intelligence and reverence, then "our labor is not in vain" (1 Corinthians 15:58). My goal in writing this book was not merely that one would buy it, but that the reader would be transformed by the God of the author. Amen.